T0287406

THE
GOLDEN
TOUCH

Celebrating 35 Years of
Penguin Random House India

Foreword by **AMITABH BACHCHAN**

THE GOLDEN TOUCH

The Journey of Kalyan Jewellers

An
Autobiography

T.S. KALYANARAMAN

Translated from the Malayalam by Anoop Thomas

PENGUIN
BUSINESS

An imprint of Penguin Random House

PENGUIN BUSINESS

USA | Canada | UK | Ireland | Australia
New Zealand | India | South Africa | China | Singapore

Penguin Business is part of the Penguin Random House group of companies
whose addresses can be found at global.penguinrandomhouse.com

Published by Penguin Random House India Pvt. Ltd
4th Floor, Capital Tower 1, MG Road,
Gurugram 122 002, Haryana, India

First published in Malayalam as *Athmavishvasam* by Mathrubhumi Books, Kozhikode, 2022
This hardcover edition published in Penguin Business by Penguin Random House India 2023

Copyright © T.S. Kalyanaraman 2023
Translation copyright © Anoop Thomas 2023

Photographs courtesy of T.S. Kalyanaraman

All rights reserved

10 9 8 7 6 5 4 3

The views and opinions expressed in this book are the author's own and the
facts are as reported by him which have been verified to the extent possible,
and the publishers are not in any way liable for the same.

ISBN 9780670098798

Typeset in Adobe Garamond Pro by Manipal Technologies Limited, Manipal
Printed at Replika Press Pvt. Ltd, India

This book is sold subject to the condition that it shall not, by way of trade
or otherwise, be lent, resold, hired out, or otherwise circulated without the
publisher's prior consent in any form of binding or cover other than that in
which it is published and without a similar condition including this condition
being imposed on the subsequent purchaser.

www.penguin.co.in

Contents

A m i t a b h   B a c h c h a n

4th August 2021

Somewhere about 2000 years ago, a young boy called Adi Shankaracharya, rose like a phoenix in the skies of what was beginning to seem like the sunset of a civilization before him. He crafted a systematic vision for mankind to rise above mundane, temporal livelihoods to the transcendental glory of being human. His Advait philosophy remains even to date the most enduring quest of mankind in every way of life...

If I were to place a template of success for any start-up today, discounting the support and encouragement provided by governments and the administration today, I would still say the first of those systematic templates was crafted by Adi Shankaracharya. And, if you cannot find that template, I strongly recommend this autobiography of Mr. T.S. Kalyanaraman or Swamy, as he is lovingly called. I think, Swamy is for start-ups today, what Adi Shankaracharya was for Advait.

The story of Kalyan Jewellers and the life of Swamy are quite simply inseparable. And, methinks, it is a handbook for entrepreneurs who venture into the world of start-ups today, if only for the vision, the mission, the belief, the determination and the persistence required in some of the toughest conditions.

An enterprise, a business, is many a times the only lifeline for its originator. One makes it the primary purpose of life. And thus a lifetime goes into its making. If you were to ask the person after it's all done and dusted, I'm not sure it's possible to remember every detail. These things just happen, like a raging wind blowing over the water and land without the resistance of any boundaries.

The faith in the goodness of human societies, the belief in the economy of happiness, and the urge to add value to the wealth of human efforts at progress are perhaps the most outstanding features of TSK's vision.

A business is not merely about managing its assets or its growth. I feel, its more about steering a vision beyond visible horizons, and also daring to keep driving in the most uncertain terrains.

Janak B/2 V L Mehta Road Juhu Mumbai 400 049
(Res) 91-22-2613 1007 (Off) 91-22-2611 4016   abcl@bom3.vsnl.net.in

Amitabh Bachchan

There was a time in the past when Gold, Silver and gems were the only currency for econom. exchange. And, it wasn't very long ago in India when there was more jewellery in the people homes than there was with the government. आपत्तधनं it was called in the house - wealth to b used only in a crisis.

Gold, Silver and precious stones have become a commodity only after printed currency, an now currency as digital numbers on computers, have replaced them to accommodate the larg volume of industrial activities, and the relative valuation of currencies among various nations

Yet, even today, jewelry still remains आपत्तधनं in every household. It's a commodity which car be converted to money like any permanent asset, and its value varies only with demand anc supply, not with depreciation. Jewelry does not depreciate like technology.

The story of Kalyan Jewelers reminds of an anecdote I had heard once. Two salesmen of a shoe factory visit a new territory where no one wears shoes. One of them comes back dejected, that there is no market for shoes because no one wears shoes in the place. The other salesmen come back all thrilled that no one wears shoes, that there is a new market for the shoes!

TSK, I think, is the second kind of salesman. At a time when Indians were only keeping jewelry at home, and when jewelry was considered the equivalent of currency, TSK saw an emerging commodity market of jewelry. And, what's more, gave his lifetime to build a nationwide and overseas enterprise!

A verse in Sanskrit says:

यथा चतुर्भिः कनकं परीक्ष्यते निर्घषणच्छेदन तापताडनैः। तथा चतुर्भिः पुरुषः परीक्ष्यते त्यागेन शीलेन गुणेन कर्मणा॥ - सुभाषित्

Meaning, as Gold is tested for purity in four ways, by rubbing, cutting, heating and beating, so is a person tested for purity, by sacrifices, culture, qualities and work.

In the journey of the TSK family, I must say the metaphor is also literally true. The intense pursuit to guarantee the purity of the Jewels is an actual mission which matches perfectly with the family's own integrity and unwavering commitment to building trust.

And, like all good things in life, such an inspiring tradition begins at home.

Janak B/2 V. L. Mehta Road Juhu Mumbai 400 049
(Res) 91-22-2613 1007 (Off) 91-22-2611 4016 abcl@bom3.vsnl.net.in

A m i t a b h   B a c h c h a n

I might say, and this is something that I have personally observed, the pivotal role of Mrs. S. Kalyanaraman in creating and sustaining the harmony within, deserves an exclusive knowledgment and salutation. The mission and objectives of building awareness and trust in e services of Kalyan Jewelers is an offshoot of the central faith at home which has held the mily together through all the ups and downs. This credit must go to the mother of the house cause, I believe, no government or institution knows how to apply the principles of good vernance better than a mother does at home.

fact, at times, such is the binding force that a mother's mere presence can be enough to rengthen the fabric of traditions and trust.

Iere is wishing TSK, Ramesh, Rajesh, Radhika and the entire family of Kalyan Jewelers, ontinual success and growing accomplishments.

Amitabh Bachchan

Janak B/2 V L Mehta Road Juhu Mumbai 400 049
(Res) 91-22-2613 1007 (Off) 91-22-2611 4016   abcl@bom3.vsnl.net.in

Introduction

The first book I had known in my life was the Ramayana. My grandfather, who introduced me to the book, used to narrate stories from it while I listened intently. When I could read by myself, he presented me with a copy of the book. It was a sea of stories. And I stepped into it . . . I made reading a habit. How many stories! What an experience! How many lines entered my heart! The varied conversations . . . But, never have I wanted to write something on my own. And it might surprise you when someone like me comes before you with his autobiography. The more I think about it, the more I find it hard to believe—how it happened. The Covid years, which shook the world, might have been a reason.

Hardly had 2020 begun than a virus, which came from China, no larger than a grain of sand, multiplied and wreaked havoc on the world. We lost sleep over voices crying hoarse about 'Corona' and 'Covid'. Scared of the uninvited guest knocking at the door, we stayed indoors.

Since the virus rapidly spread through contact, countries felt that the best way to keep it under check would be a lockdown. By the end of March 2020, India was under a complete lockdown. Downing shutters and sitting idle at home were something not everyone could digest. But, as there was no other way out, people slowly adjusted themselves to the new world order.

Naturally, days of boredom followed. There was nothing much to do. One couldn't go outdoors. There were no get-togethers, weddings or birthday parties. Life was confined to the four walls of one's house, even in the villages. People for whom twenty-four hours seemed insufficient earlier did not know what to do with the time they had on their hands. Cobwebs of laziness covered every nook and cranny of one's self.

My situation, too, was no different. It was as if someone had switched off all my activities. I couldn't go to my office.

Gone were the usual business meetings. What if the car you were travelling in suddenly lost power and stalled in the middle of the road? It was very much the same situation. The flip side is I got to spend quality time with my family. But somehow my mind couldn't adjust to the massive changes in my daily routine.

I found comfort in reading books. As I am a religious person, my reading was selective. Still, I had a lot of time at my disposal and I wanted to make the most of it. But how?

As I sat back and reflected on what to do, my mind went back in time. I attempted to dust the cobwebs off memories lying in the far recesses of my mind. I rummaged through many albums, documents, drawings and paintings. I felt a lot of relief. As I began conversing with my family members about the past, I felt a sense of energy rushing through my veins.

I felt a ray of light passing through me as I spoke with family members about the past. As there was precious little to be done at home, my children and grandchildren gathered around me to hear my stories. My words seemed like the grandfather tales of yore to them.

Until then, I had kept all my memories stacked in boxes. They were all within my reach, but for some reason or the other, I never bothered to search for them. The lockdown period made me open the boxes one by one. In each box was a story. The story of my life, my experiences. A life that I had lived a long time ago.

I got them one night from a box: a couple of old notebooks. I had scribbled something in them. No, they weren't in order. Call them random musings from my experiences. I wasn't in the habit of keeping a diary. I made no notes of daily happenings. If there was something that touched my heart, I wrote that down.

I do not know when it all began. When I saw all those books, I recollected I had my memories in them. Somewhere along the line, I had lost touch with all of those. That night I realized the words I had once scribbled had life in them. They were immortal.

In them, I saw my early years—school, college and my entry into the business field. It was something only I could read and understand. Some were insignificant. There was nothing of interest to anyone. Yet, in them was my life.

I showed the notebooks to all at the family gathering the next evening. My children were surprised. My grandchildren flipped through the pages of the notebooks out of sheer curiosity. I explained to them what I had written in them. From a couple of lines, they grew to be a story. The sparkle I saw in their eyes made me want to go further into the past.

It was from that family gathering that the idea of a book took shape. 'Now, you can write an autobiography . . .' my children told me. I laughed it away. Though I took it lightly then, the idea grew on me as days passed. What the children told me began ringing in my ears constantly. 'Only famous people write autobiographies. What autobiography can a businessman like me write? Is my life that important to write an autobiography? What do I have to share with people?'

All these questions led to another question.

'Who am I?'

It is a question to which even the great sages have not found an answer. The more one thinks about it, the more an answer eludes it.

The only answer I can give is: 'I am but an ordinary human being—created by God.'

My thoughts and life are very simple. There is nothing extraordinary about them. But I have always felt the lessons my forefathers taught me are relevant even today. I wanted to share my thoughts with you. That's what led me to undertake the adventure called 'Autobiography'.

My life is not at all eventful. I began my business in textiles and moved on to jewellery. I don't have any shocking incidents to tell you. I don't have any rags-to-riches story either. So, what do you have to tell us, you may think.

Apart from my story, this is the history of Kalyan Jewellers—till the present. Between the pages, you will find some incidents in my life. That's all. Transparency and Trust. These are the two pillars on which Kalyan Jewellers exists. Repose your trust in the people and you will never know what failure is. That was the credo of my grandfather and father. That's how they did business. My self-confidence comes from them.

Never engage in cut-throat or dishonest business. Think of the people involved, in all that you do. Take them into confidence. Be trustworthy. If you follow all these rules, you can be a successful businessman. What you deserve will surely come to you. This is what I want to share with you through my book.

Let me repeat. There is nothing extraordinary about this autobiography. It's the humble desire of a businessman above seventy to share with you what he has seen, heard and learnt over the years.

Paying obeisance to Sri Ramaswamy, who has made everything possible, I gladly invite you into my life . . .

1

The Origin of Our Roots

One of my favourite pastimes is playing with my grandchildren. I'm game for their tantrums, act according to their whims and fancies, and become one among them. Never once have I felt them to be a tedious affair. It's the other way around. The child in us awakens as we grow old. Old age is the second childhood.

On one such occasion, one of my grandchildren asked me: 'Grandpa, where did we come from?' His curiosity was about the enigma called the human race. My thoughts were about my ancestors. Where do the roots of the present generation, sitting right before my eyes, lie? How did we spread roots in this place called Punkunnam in Thrissur?

This is what I told my grandchildren: 'Each one of us is a tree. Do you know how a tree manages to stand upright without falling? Isn't it because of its roots? All human beings have roots. The roots of human beings are their ancestors—grandfathers, grandmothers, great-grandfathers, great-grandmothers . . . Though you are small children, you have them too—invisible roots. Your ancestors, who are long gone, are your roots. It is from them that we sprang forth as trees . . .'

I don't know whether my grandson who asked the question or those who sat around me understood what I said. I don't know whether they were satisfied with my answer. But, for me, it was a journey back in time—to my ancestors. That day, all my thoughts were about them.

I remember my grandfather telling me that our forefathers fled from Tamil Nadu and came to Kerala via Palakkad. Along with them was a seven-year-old boy. He was stranded when the rest of the crowd went their different ways. Not knowing where to go, he wandered till he came to the Triprayar temple. Tired, he fainted. When he woke up, he stretched out his hand for the *prasadam* (sacred food from the temple). The boy's name was Rama Shastri. The sacred ground of Lord Rama had indeed become a haven for the young Rama!

As days passed, the boy caught the attention of those performing pujas and rituals at the temple. They inquired about his past. Moved by his story, they asked him to stay on to 'distribute prasadam'. Soon, the boy began distributing prasadam at the Triprayar temple. With Lord Rama's blessings, the boy soon endeared himself to all he came across.

Rama Shastri belonged to a family with a rich astrological tradition. It was no wonder he inherited the tradition from his forefathers. Several hands stretch forth daily to receive the prasadam. Though Rama used to look at the lines on the outstretched palms, he did not read them.

When he was fourteen, the temple folks took up the responsibility of finding a bride for Rama Shastri. By that time, he had become the darling of not just them but all those who came to the temple. He won people's hearts with his congenial nature and gentle conversations. Many considered him a member of their own family.

The temple authorities found a bride for the young Rama Shastri. The first attempt came a cropper. The search continued till they came across a girl from a very poor family. Luckily, the horoscopes matched. After the wedding, Rama Shastri and his wife settled down in a thatched house at nearby Trikkur. Rama soon became the *kazhakam* (staffer) of Cherpu temple.

Sitarama Iyer, my great-grandfather, was their eldest son. When he came of age, he was made the *karyasthan* (administrator) of the temple. In those days, the temple was in disarray and had only a meagre revenue. Under Sitarama Iyer, who was renowned for his hard work and trustworthiness, the dark clouds disappeared and the temple prospered.

In those days, the land was ruled by the royal family. The maharaja used to recognize and reward honest people. As a token of appreciation for restoring the temple that was falling into ruins to its lost glory, the maharaja appointed my grandfather's father (Sitarama Iyer) as its manager. The post was known as *pattali*. With that, my grandfather's family became close to the maharaja. Along with the recognition, the maharaja presented him with a golden *Veera Sringala* (one belonging to the valiant chain).

My grandfather, Kalyanarama Iyer, was Sitarama Iyer's second son. Trikkur Sitarama Iyer's son, Kalyanarama Iyer, later came to be known as T.S. Kalyanarama Iyer. The word 'Kalyan' has its origins in my grandfather's name.

Our hallmarks—honesty, transparency and trust—which we so closely consider sacred even to this day, have their origins in Rama Shastri, the seven-year-old boy who came all by himself from Tamil Nadu to Triprayar via Palakkad. His son, Sitarama Iyer, who followed in his footsteps held the family hallmarks close to his heart. The one word our forefathers passed on from one generation to another is—trust. It is this intrinsic quality they breathed into successive generations. It is this flame our forefathers kindled in them. Like self-confidence.

Ramachandra Iyer was Sitarama Iyer's brother—my great-grandfather's younger brother. Academically brilliant, he took a barrister's degree, became a renowned lawyer and settled down in Madras. He was conferred with the title of 'Diwan Peshkar Ramachandra Iyer'.

Though he had settled down in Madras, Ramachandra Iyer would often come to Trikkur. Legend has it he had a revelation at Triprayar temple while going from Trikkur to Vadakkunnathan temple to offer his prayers. The godly voice had told him to construct a small temple dedicated to Sri Rama.

The title of Diwan Bahadur came as a blessing in disguise for Ramachandra Iyer. The maharaja gifted him with free land! It was on this land that he constructed the Sri Rama temple. Soon, he built a house near the temple. That was how the temple village of Pushpagiri sprang up.

The family moved to Pushpagiri when my grandfather passed the Intermediate course. Among the brothers, only my grandfather and his elder brother, Balarama Iyer, were educated. Ramachandra Iyer looked after their education.

In the midst of all this was his daughter Bhuvaneshwari's wedding. A huge *pandal* (tent) was erected near the temple for the wedding. The wedding was a grand affair. When it was time to dismantle the pandal, my grandfather and his brother approached Ramachandra Iyer with a request: 'Though we have completed our studies, we have not found employment. We'd like to do something for a living. Kindly permit us to set up a handloom mill . . .' My grandfather was a Gandhian. Lofty ideals and self-confidence were the warp and the woof with which he strived to weave a fine fabric of life.

Ramachandra Iyer agreed. Soon, Punkunnam resounded with the sounds of Sitaram Mills. The name has its origins in the name of my grandfather's father, Sitaram Iyer. Hence, the name Sitaram Mills. I can see a doubt arising in the minds of some of my readers: 'Sitaram Mills—the name rings a bell. How is that related to the Kalyan family?' Yes, your doubt is indeed right. The name Sitaram Mills has a prominent place in Kerala politics. The first strides of K. Karunakaran, the Bheeshmacharya of Kerala politics, were from Sitaram Mills. The mill has been witness to many political developments. It was from this landmark mill, very much a part of the Kerala fabric, that the first textiles of Kalyan, the business house, rolled out.

2

Honesty Is the Best Policy

One must have a knack for doing business. A businessman will always see what others don't. His eyes will forever be focused on profits. As such, he may lose sight of many important aspects of life—the state of others' lives, sentiments and even his own life.

The general belief is that to be truly successful in business, one must always have one's eyes fixed on profits. But it was not so for my grandfather, whom I am named after. He did not start the weaving mills with an eye on profit. He was a simple Gandhian with compassionate eyes. How could such a person be successful in business? It was very difficult in those days.

But my grandfather did honest business. By doing so, he was proving that one could do business successfully and make profits without having an eye on them. One could read it from his face!

Ramachandra Iyer provided the capital required to set up the weaving mill. The business prospered in no time, thanks to Lord Rama's blessings and my grandfather's honesty. If my memory is correct, there were over 1000 workers in the mill. Since the eldest brother had a revered position in the family, the business was headed by my grandfather's eldest brother Balarama Iyer. My grandfather managed the business. Shortly after turning sixty, Balarama Iyer passed away and his children joined the business. My grandfather decided to move on to textile retailing and set up a small textile shop, T.S. Kalyanarama Iyer Textiles, near Thrissur District Hospital.

Though he was short of funds, my grandfather had no difficulty in getting loans as he knew a lot of cloth dealers. That was indeed a big relief for him. With the little help he got from them, he was able to open his shop and do business.

In those days, the largest textile shop in Thrissur was Chakola Textiles and they were an established retailer. Hence, my grandfather's business was dull. My grandfather had a huge family comprising four boys and six girls. Despite hardships, he was not one to let go of that intrinsic quality called honesty. He swore by it and lived by it. Trust—it meant the whole world to him. Never once did he try to do business by dishonest means, cheat the buyers by increasing the price of his textiles or sell old stuff.

He held steadfast to his principles even when poverty stared him in the face. One day, my grandfather prayed to Lord Rama: 'My children will starve if I go on like this. I will pave the roof of the temple at Punkunnam with copper if you help me improve my business.' It was a heart-wrenching prayer. A way opened before my grandfather, though it's wrong to say it was because of the prayer. The World War broke out ten days after his prayer. Let me make myself very clear. The World War did not break out because of his prayer! Rather, my grandfather benefited from the World War.

Clothes were scarce when the war broke out. It is said cloth that was sold for as low as one naya paisa was sold for as high as Re 1! With that, the financial position of my grandfather improved. As promised, he paved the roof of Punkunnam temple with copper. From then on, his fortunes increased.

But my grandfather's status never went from poor to wealthy. He always tried to set apart his income for the poor—even when his financial position was bad. 'Let's share what we have' was what he used to say. Not much food was cooked at home in those days. He disliked wasting food. So, only what was required at home was cooked. Food was served to whoever came home hungry. That was when he said, 'Let's share what we have.' He gave away whatever he had with him if someone approached him for financial help. Haven't you heard of Karna's generosity? My grandfather was as generous as Karna.

I remember distinctly the days I spent with my grandfather. He was a Gandhian to the core. He never spoke on Sundays. On certain days, he used to call me to his side and teach me lessons from the Ramayana. He passed away when I was studying for my pre-degree. I am happy that I could spend my entire childhood with him. I used to sleep with my grandfather at night. I can say with confidence and pride that I learnt the basics of business from him. No, it was not a textbook-like lesson to make a profit. Rather, it was a smooth flow of thoughts on how to do honest business.

'We don't want any secrets in business.' This was what my grandfather always told me. You don't need brains to do business. Our honesty is more than enough. There must be transparency in all that we do. We mustn't hide anything from those who come to buy our products. We must meet all their requirements. If they say something nasty, we must listen patiently and not lose our cool.

In no way should we think of profits. Reduce the price as much as you can. This way, the turnover will increase. When the turnover increases, your income also rises and your coffers will always be full. Dishonesty will lead to your downfall. This was my grandfather's credo.

Not just this. He told me many more things. 'Never let go of Sri Rama, the poor or our business.' This was the sacred mantra he whispered into my ears—something that I still keep close to my heart as a priceless treasure.

Sri Rama is our eternal guardian. Who else can be the best example of honesty other than Dasharatha's son—the noble soul who was ready to sacrifice everything to uphold the truth? During my grandfather's time, it was customary to offer food (*nivedyam*) daily to the deity of the Punkunnam temple. Today, we ourselves have become offerings to the Lord.

Service was my grandfather's second credo. Do business. But see to it that it's a service too to the people. Think of the poor when you do business and also when you get the returns. He always advised us to hold on tight to the three cardinal values: honesty, trust and transparency. Money will come to you automatically if you stick to these principles, he said. The people will give it to you.

Grandfather never used to pile up his money. Only very little money was needed for household expenses. Food was in plenty. So were jackfruits and mangoes. One only needed to step out into the sprawling farm to gather what was needed for a sumptuous meal every day. There was no need to go shopping for supplies.

Grandfather had moved into the house he had constructed near Sitaram Mills. Temple, prayers, business—this was his daily routine. He never considered those who worked in the mill as workers. Rather, he considered them as his siblings. There were two people his age—Kochu and Velu. Though they had retired from service, grandfather paid them a salary till their death.

Grandfather entered politics at one stage in his life. A Gandhian, he served the public by doing good deeds without hurting anyone—thereby winning over their hearts. He was elected unopposed. As municipal chairman of Thrissur, he devoted his time to serving the people.

Later, he started a wholesale textile shop on Post Office Road. That's the nature of roots. They keep growing.

3

The Practical School

My grandfather had four sons. The eldest among them was my father, Sitarama Iyer. According to our family custom, the eldest grandchild gets the grandfather's name. That's how I was named T.S. Kalyanaraman. How I got my name is interesting. I received my grandfather's initials (my father is Sitaram Iyer and my grandfather, Trikkur Sitaram Iyer).

My father had nine siblings—three brothers: Pattabhirama Iyer, Ramachandran and Anantharaman, and six sisters: Thankam Ammal, Sitalakshmi, Sharadambal, Jayalakshmi, Rajalakshmi and Bhuvaneshwari. Of them, Thankam Ammal had passed away before my birth. My father was the first among the four brothers to follow in the footsteps of my grandfather in doing business. After completing their studies, the others too went their different ways. Pattabhirama Iyer left for Coimbatore to manage the Mettur Chemicals agency's affairs. He later opened his own textile shop and settled down there. While Ramachandran looked after the shop near the hospital, Anantharaman was in charge of the wholesale shop on Post Office Road. My father trod an altogether different path. Though initially, he was in the textile shop with my grandfather, he later bought a company dealing in roofing tiles—the Cochin Power Industry. There was a great demand for roofing tiles. My father diversified his business by buying the tile company.

During this time, my father got married. My mother, Narayani Ammal, hailed from a not-so-well-to-do family in Payyannur. Her parents are Krishna Iyer and Lakshmi.

I was born on 23 April 1947, under the Rohini star. The day was unique. It was Akshaya Tritiya! Let there be a golden glow in his life, the gods may have thought. Maybe that's why I was lucky to have been born on the auspicious day of Akshaya Tritiya—a day closely associated with gold.

My memory takes me as far as Class III. Though ours was a huge joint family, we lived as one unit. Call it a harmonious piece of music with absolutely no discordant notes. I used to play with my cousins. Though we had our share of quarrels and fights, we settled things among ourselves. Unlike today, parents in those days never interfered in the disputes of their children and made mountains out of molehills. The squabbles were mostly about a mango or a sweet. Or about not allowing one to take part in a game. It is when the elders in the joint family poke their noses into the matter that the issue takes a turn for the worse. Our fights normally began and ended with ourselves. A dispute lasted only for as long as the sweet in question dissolved in the mouth!

My father has seven children. I am the eldest. I have four brothers: Anantharaman, Pattabhiraman, Balaraman, Ramachandran, and two sisters: Meenakshi and Geethalakshmi. We used to sit on the ground and have food with our grandfather before leaving for school. There was no formal breakfast. We had either rice or rice gruel in the morning, a practice we continue even to this day. I still have my meals around 10.30 a.m. before leaving for the office.

Despite having meals in the morning, we would all be hungry by noon. To satiate our hunger, my father arranged food for us daily at Mani's Cafe, near our school. When the bell rang at noon, we went to Mani's Cafe to have our food.

I went to Model School and have vivid memories of an incident that happened while studying in Class III. One day, Sitaram Mills caught fire. The flames that had broken out in the morning continued late into the night. It was as if a thousand torches were lit at once. A wall separated the mill and our house. The fire could have entered our house at any time. A fire raged within our hearts as we stood there. What raised our concern was a haystack near the house. What if a spark ignited the entire haystack? All the elders of the house waited with bated breath and vessels of water, ready to meet any eventuality. None of us slept that day. How could we, when the flames burned bright in front of our eyes?

My father sent me to the textile shop near the hospital when I reached Class VII. It was an act akin to a child taking its first step. I had to go to the shop on all holidays. The reward was a masala dosa, either from Mani's Cafe or Pathan's Hotel.

I was not required to work at the shop. All I had to do was simply stand behind the counter, observe everything and exchange pleasantries with those who came to the shop. What my father required of me at that tender age was nothing but an interaction with the world.

'Swamikutty, why are you looking so glum today? Didn't you get masala dosa today?' some would ask. That question used to give me some respite from hunger. Some merely smiled, while others tweaked my cheeks playfully enough to make me happy and contented.

People from all walks of life came to our shop—people with different temperaments. Each one had a style of his or her own. The counter was a classroom to study people.

Our shop was small with a daily sales turnover of Rs 3000. It was a pretty good sum in the 1960s. I was given strenuous work when my 'counter training' was over. One such job was to untie the cloth from the board. My hands hurt, but the thought of masala dosa eased the pain.

My next job was to cut the cloth, foot by foot. My hands ached. The blisters on my palms are testimony to the great lessons I've learnt in life. The thickening of the skin on my palms was, in fact, chapters of life firmly etched in my mind.

The shop near the hospital had only four workers when I went there for the first time. There wasn't much cloth to be sold. The most important among them was the Jagannathan Mull (type of fabric). We had a unique variety too—cloth from Binny company, something only our shop had. Getting the dealership of Binny was a great achievement in those days.

Though three or four shops had functioned in Thrissur, none had Binny cloth. So, after purchasing cloth and materials from other shops, people came to our shop only to buy Binny cloth. The blue and the khaki Binny cloth with which school students and the police stitched their uniforms, respectively, bore a very high standard, which was why it was in great demand. Though the demand was high, the supply was low. Each distributor got only two or three spools of fabric.

My tender mind developed a dislike towards people who came to our shop only to buy Binny cloth. What was the need to give our prized possession to those who came to our shop after making purchases at other shops? Only those people who purchased other varieties of cloth from our shop should be given the rare Binny fabric, I felt. I conveyed my opinion to my father. He was furious. You must give the customer what he asks for, he said.

My father had a Landmaster car, which was always jam-packed with five to ten people. There were only horse carriages during his childhood. So, when he bought a car, it became an object of amusement. People would stand and gaze at the tortoise-like car as it rolled through the roads.

In the evenings, my father would come from the tile company to the shop near the hospital and scrutinize the accounts. If I was there in the shop, he would inquire about the day's news. Later, as promised, we would go hand in hand to Mani's Cafe to savour the masala dosa.

My father silently taught me many things. His life was his message—a lesson through which he taught us how to live in this world. Father, to us, was not the stick-bearing strict disciplinarian who taught us life's great lessons by striking fear in our minds. Rather, he led us on the right path through love and affection. I was an average student. Never once did he chide me or beat me for scoring low marks. I was fond of badminton, football, cricket and the theatre. My father encouraged all these activities. I feel a certain warmth at the tips of my fingers when I think about my father. For it was he who led me by the hand down many lanes. His fingers had a special warmth. To see my father, I only need to close my eyes.

My mother wasn't so well-educated, but she managed a large joint family and was particular that not a murmur of discontent was heard within our home. Mother would wait for us with our food, however late we came in. During the Onam season, we would reach home only around 1 a.m. after winding up our business for the day, only to find our mother fully awake and waiting for us. If memories about my father radiate warmth, memories of my mother are like the touch of the cool wind. On days when I arrived late from the shop, my mother would make me lie down on her lap and caress my weary head. Like a soothing lullaby, a cool feeling would encompass my entire body from head to toe, and I would soon fall asleep. How I wish I could lie down on her lap again!

* * *

After my Class VII studies were over, I went to the shop even during the midsummer vacation. Though at first I was led by hopes of getting a masala dosa, it later gave way to a sense of duty. Doing business energized me and gave me immense pleasure. During Onam season, I would try my hand at the fabric spool. Though my hands developed blisters and the skin peeled away, I knew no pain. For I was gaining rich experience—one that filled my heart with pride. Lost in work and the heavy rush at the shop, time simply flew by.

Speaking with those who thronged our shop gave me immense joy. 'Swamikutty . . .' I used to feel a wave of love and affection engulfing me when they addressed me thus.

I was an average student. I have said this earlier. But my love for mathematics helped me a lot in the shop. I managed the accounts manually in the beginning. Later, I took help from the 'ready reckoner'. My father, who came in the evenings, taught me the dos and don'ts of business and how to differentiate between right and wrong. I consider this my greatest asset. All the practical lessons I learnt in my childhood from that small shop have held me in good stead—even to this day. I firmly believe that an hour's conversation with a person who had come to the shop would give you greater management lessons than what can be found in any of the management books in the world. In the world of business, the consumer is said to be king. But rather than seeing consumers as kings with the all-powerful crown and sceptre, I'd like to revere them as gurus who teach us valuable lessons.

Not all people are alike. Each one has a different character. We may not approve of their actions. But each one teaches us a lesson. That's how all consumers, good or bad, become our gurus.

The greatest lesson we gain from consumers is practical knowledge. It's priceless. I firmly believe in practical knowledge. The knowledge I've gained in life is not from classrooms or management institutes. What I consider my wealth is the knowledge I've gained through experience and the words of wisdom from my forefathers. This gave me self-confidence.

No child in the family came to the shop before completing Class VII. Once here, the shop became his second classroom. I came first. My brothers followed suit.

When I reached Class X, I was influenced by something that was to have a permanent effect on me later in life—yoga. It became a daily routine, a way of life; something I practise even to this day. My guru was Sahasrabuddha who had come from Delhi to Thrissur to teach yoga. He was conducting a week-long course. I joined the course for the heck of it. I had very little knowledge of what it was, its nuances, purpose or benefits. When the course was over, I was a different person. However, I continued learning yoga in my hometown in the classes conducted by V.R. Iyer.

Yoga is now a part of me. I feel I'm lacking in something if I don't practise yoga. I begin my day with yoga. The positive energy it gives keeps me going for an entire day. I have never given it a miss since the day I mastered yoga. It had been so even on the day of my children's weddings.

Something else happened when I reached Class X. My learning process during the vacation shifted to our wholesale shops on Post Office Road. By that time, fashion too had undergone a sea change. Single-colour shirts became the order of the day. Saris and skirts sported floral patterns.

4

Old Habits Die Hard

Adolescence is the most important chapter in a person's life. For many, it's a time to celebrate. But, since my heart was in our business, I never felt like celebrating the occasion like others did.

I did my pre-degree (commerce) and degree courses (BCom) at Kerala Varma College. Whenever there was a strike, I went straight to our shop. It was the same during the holidays. Yet, my interest in badminton, football and mono acting from my school days never waned. On certain days, I'd choose games over the business and skip going to our shop. My father never objected to this.

My grandfather died while I was doing my pre-degree course. The end of a great legacy, so we felt. It was as if the root of our family tree had disappeared into the ground, never to be seen again. But not before energizing the other roots that had come from it. My grandfather continued to live on through my father and his brothers.

An incident deeply hurt me, the pain of which still lingers. One of my classmates was Johnson. Tough and efficient, he was the captain of our hockey team and leader of the National Cadet Corps (NCC). He was our hero.

The Indo-Pak war was on. Johnson was among the NCC cadets who opted to go to the war front. Sadly, he never returned. A rifle shot ended his life. I still have vivid memories of the brave soul who moved about on our college campus like a hero . . .

My passion for acting stands out among my activities during college life. I loved mono acting and, most often, won prizes for it. My father was the inspiration behind my interest in acting and films. He used to take us to all the movies during my childhood. The two prominent theatres of those days were Rama Varma and Jose.

My father was an ardent fan of Sivaji Ganesan movies. He loved MGR, Sathyan and Prem Nazir. We would huddle ourselves in our father's car and go as soon as a movie hit the silver screen.

My mother's hometown of Payyanur too played a not-too-insignificant role in developing my passion for acting. Plays were enacted on a huge stage next to the maidan near the Subramanya Swami temple. In my childhood, I used to go to my mother's hometown during the holidays and watch the plays that were staged every night. Troupes from Payyanur used to bag prizes in almost all the plays staged at the drama competitions. Inspired by what I saw on stage, I took to acting.

College life was interesting. I used to go to college on foot while studying for the pre-degree course. I switched to riding bicycles while studying for a degree. I can distinctly recall the faces of all my teachers: Kuruppal Master, P.T. Master Kuriappan Sir, Mariamma Teacher, Lakshmi Teacher, K.P.R. Menon Sir . . . most of them aren't alive today. Whenever time permits, I visit my old teachers and I become that young college student again.

I graduated in 1971. By the end of the year, my father and his brothers had agreed on the partition of properties. As his share, my father got the tile company and the textile shop near the hospital. During this time, my family was looking to get me married, and that's how Ramadevi, who has roots in Thrissur, entered my life.

Rama's father's family belonged to Nellayi and her mother's family to Thrissur. Rama stayed with her parents in Madras (presently

Chennai). Her father, M.S. Venkitaraman, was the general manager of Esso Oil Company (known as Burmah Shell in India) and was stationed in Karachi.

Rama was only fifteen when our marriage was finalized! She was junior to me by nine years. My father desired to set up a textile shop for each one of his children. He had begun the groundwork for his dream project soon after my engagement. That's how a new textile shop sprang up on Municipal Office Road on 17 May 1972. Playback singer Yesudas inaugurated it.

Yesudas and Rama's father were next-door neighbours in Madras and close friends. Rama's father let Yesudas use his car occasionally; such was the bond between the two families. Since Rama's father had lost touch with the state, he did not know lakhs of music lovers worshipped Yesudas in Kerala.

My father wanted Yesudas to inaugurate the shop. He approached Rama's father, who was glad to help him. To Rama's father, it was child's play—maybe because he was ignorant of the intrinsic value of a great music idol as Yesudas or because of his bonds with his great friend. Rama's father helped my father fulfil his heart's desire.

Rama's father realized the popularity of Yesudas in Kerala only when he saw the huge crowd that thronged the area to have a mere glimpse of their favourite singer. After the inaugural function, Yesudas returned to Chennai, but not before rendering an immensely popular film song: *Kaattile Paazhmulam Thandil Ninnum* . . . Truly, a melodious opening!

I got married on 3 July 1972. Yesudas graced our wedding with his presence and enriched it with his choicest renderings. Rama stayed back in Madras to complete her studies as she was still a student. Six months later, she made her grand entry into our large family.

Close on the heels of opening our shop, we bought a car. It was my first vehicle—a second-hand Ambassador: KRH 7082. It belonged to the owner of Thrissur Woodlands Hotel on MG Road. I did not employ a driver; I drove it myself.

Though my father had set up the textile shop for me, he did not hand over the entire responsibility of running it to me. He would come to the shop by 5 p.m. and stay there till 8 p.m. He would keenly observe my performance and how I dealt with the customers. He would closely examine my purchases and sales down to the last rupee and correct me if I erred. When he was confident I could handle everything efficiently, he left the entire responsibility of running the business to me. We had seven employees and approximate daily sales worth Rs 10,000.

Kalyanram Textiles. That was the name of the shop. It became Kalyan Textiles after four or five years. Kalyan, the name now synonymous with trust the world over, was the brainchild of my father, who had very little exposure to the world. He must have hit upon that name when all the gods were showering their choicest blessings on him.

Though the shop was set up for me, all my brothers used to come there and help me. Here too, we were one family. It never occurred to me that it was 'my shop' or to my brothers that it was 'his shop'. It never ought to be like that was what our father taught us right from childhood.

I had said earlier that my father desired to set up a shop for each one of us. By 1974–75, my second brother got a shop. The following year, my third brother had a shop. In five years, all five of us had our shops. My father used to visit each shop for overall supervision.

Those days, the leading newspaper in Thrissur was *Express*. We would place full-page advertisements for all five of our shops in *Express* on all Sundays. The rate for a full-page advertisement was Rs 10,000. We used to make an annual payment for all the advertisements. Looking back, I feel my father was years ahead in successfully experimenting with business strategies.

* * *

'The best textiles at reasonable prices.' This was how we advertised our products. We had dedicated customers. I had a personal rapport with all of them—something I learnt when I was in Class VII while being at the counter of the textile shop.

I still remember the names of many people who used to frequent our shop: Krishnakumar, Velappan, Antony, Johnson, Peter, municipality employee Rama, Lalitha, Hemambika . . . The employees of the police station and P&T department would come straight to our shop as soon as they got their salaries on the first of every month. Buying new clothes every month was a habit in those days. By then, newer fashions in sarees and shirtings would arrive at our shop.

A festive mood pervaded the place. More than the pressure of doing business, those days presented us with the warmth of friendship. Those doing business in the neighbourhood would come to our shop to take a break. I used to go to their shops too. Our neighbours were the Ayurveda shop of Chandrika Soaps, P.C. Medicals, Jaya Bakery, Fancy Fabrics and Tradelinks. On days when we had free time, we would gather in one shop and exchange pleasantries. We used to talk about local and world affairs. In the evenings, we used to meet in front of the Vadakkunnathan temple. Don't present-day friends meet in groups? We were like that back in the olden days.

I wouldn't say we were very shrewd in doing business those days. We did business by imbibing the lessons our grandfather and father taught us. If someone came to our shop saying the colour of their clothes faded, we would give them fresh ones. It was the same whenever a customer came to our shop with worn-out clothes. Never compromise on quality was what our forefathers taught us. If we found any one piece lacking in quality, we returned the entire lot to the company. These were things no one ever did.

Which is why I said we never used to do shrewd business. Rather, it was from our hearts. We never ran into losses as we never did cut-throat business. From a daily sales turnover of Rs 10,000, we reached Rs 25,000 in four to five years. On festive days, it soared to Rs 50,000. The reason? We offered the best service to our customers. Our business flourished with the rise in the number of regular customers.

Soon, we began a separate section for wedding sarees. To borrow a modern marketing term, our unique selling point (USP) was trust. We never tried to sell our old stock. In the textile business, it's the easiest way to make money. We sold only fresh items.

It is from that humble shop in front of the municipal office that I began my business journey. That shop is still there. The employees too. It isn't easy to forget one's humble past. Didn't I take my baby steps from there?

5

Spend Wisely

One of the happiest moments in my life happened in 1975. Into our world came a bundle of joy—our firstborn! I felt a sense of achievement the day he came into our life. It's a time when our lives take on a new meaning. It's that moment when love turns into compassion. No love is sufficient for them. And so our quest for more love begins.

It was the same feeling when our second son was born in 1978 and our daughter in 1989. Children give a new meaning to the word 'father'. They give us new insights into life. We see things from a different perspective. We open our eyes and begin to see things we had ignored all along.

We named our eldest son Rajesh. The second one was Ramesh and our daughter, Radhika. If you ask me what is my greatest asset, I'd tell you it's my family.

Selecting materials for one's shop is an art. It is up to you to purchase all the materials for the shop, my father had said in 1972 while setting it up. In the beginning, we used to buy materials from Bangalore (present-day Bengaluru) and Madras (now Chennai). By 1977–78, we began going to Bombay (now Mumbai). We journeyed by train, in the third-class compartment. In Bombay, we stayed at Hotel Adarsh on Kalbadevi Road. There was just one bathroom for all the occupants!

I had to undergo a lot of hardships in life. Only, they were at my father's insistence. He lived by his principles in business. On a personal note, he would gladly give away anything if one asked for it. He would readily part with everything he had. But nothing of that sort in business. In business, discipline mattered most.

That's why in the early years, our father asked us to travel in a third-class compartment and stay in a hotel having only a common bathroom. That was all we could afford with the profit from our Bombay purchases.

Soon, we started purchasing from Bhiwandi also. In Bhiwandi, we paid only Rs 12 for the material we used to buy for Rs 25 in Bombay. The reason? The mills in Bhiwandi did not have to pay excise duty, whereas the power looms in Bombay had to!

This business trick yielded results. Our profits increased. We began travelling in AC compartments and staying in hotels with better facilities. All this was with our father's knowledge. He was never against a change in lifestyle when business prospered and profits increased.

While I journeyed by train, many businessmen of that time travelled by plane to Bombay. *Why can't I too travel by plane*, I thought. I expressed my desire to my father. 'Travel by plane if you so wish. I have no objection to it. Only, you must benefit from the trip and recover the expenses through business.' My father agreed to the proposal when he was convinced that the profits got by purchasing materials from Bhiwandi and the recovery of expenses from the travel by plane were in line with his policy of doing business.

And so, for the first time in my life, I travelled by plane in 1982. The airfare was Rs 480. I boarded the aircraft from the Naval airport in Cochin (present Kochi). My father did not permit me to take a taxi from Trichur (currently Thrissur) to the airport, as the expense would have to be borne from our profit. 'Take the bus that leaves Trichur for the airport at 5 a.m.,' he said. I reached the bus stand at 4.45 a.m. The bus departed at 5 a.m. for the airport. From the airport, I boarded the aircraft to Bombay. The travel through the sky amidst the floating clouds was a great experience.

My father was neither a miser nor one who went after massive profits. Which is why I could easily make sense of what he meant by asking me to take the bus instead of a taxi to the airport. He knew the value of money down to the single paisa. It is this value that he taught his children.

Business is like a house of cards that can collapse at any moment. A spendthrift and his money are soon parted. In fact, extravagance leads to the downfall of any business. My father knew this very well. Spend your money wisely and you can spend it for a longer time. This was my father's credo.

During the mid-1980s, we disposed of our second-hand Ambassador car and bought a brand new Maruti 800, the latest entrant in the market and a rage those days.

Initially, there was only a trickle of customers to the shop. So, we had ample time to speak to each one who came there. It was through such conversations that we developed a bond with our customers. 'Swami, please excuse this time too. Too many expenses . . . running short of cash . . . will pay you in full next time,' some of our customers used to say. We said nothing but sent them away with a smile.

My father was against lending money to people. He had his own reasons. If you lend money, you will lose the money and the customer, he used to say. For the person who borrowed the money will neither return it nor come to the shop again.

Buying materials on credit was not his policy. Pay ready cash and take the goods was what he said. Your mental tension increases when you buy materials on credit. The thought of having to pay up eventually will affect your entire system, and this will lead to great trouble.

'Suppose you want to buy materials worth Rs 50,000. But you have at your disposal only Rs 5000. So, what do you do? Buy materials only with what you have in your hand.' This is what he taught us. During the Onam season, you may need to purchase materials worth

Rs 15 lakh. But if you have only a lesser amount with you, buy only for that amount. Never buy anything on credit.' This was my father's strict order.

'When you make a purchase, always settle the payment in full as soon as you have taken stock of the materials. There must not be a single moment's delay,' were his words. Father used to follow up his words with an inspection. We had to maintain a book and record the transactions down to the last detail—the day and date on which the materials arrived, particulars of payment, including the day and date, cheque numbers and so forth.

We used to hide certain bills from Father's vigilant eyes. We could keep payment pending on those bills for two or three days. But Father would have none of that. He would examine each drawer of the table, come up with the bills and reprimand us. He wouldn't rest until we had settled the bills in full the same day.

During this time, Father's tile factory downed its shutters. The universal reason: labour unrest. The workers were determined to bring my father to his knees. He closed it down as he was not in a position then to cede to their demands. And so, the tile factory became part of my memory.

The partition of our shops was completed in 1985. Though each of us got our share, all of us stayed in the same old house. There were ten to fifteen children, including my children and my brother's children. Our wives, father, mother . . . it was one huge family. But we lived as one, just as it was during the time of my grandfather. Unity was the foundation of our family.

Two years later, my father constructed a house for each one of us. He was particular that he should fulfil his responsibilities at the earliest. He knew what had to be done and when. As the eldest son, I got the ancestral house along with 50 cents of land.

My mother passed away in 1988. She was only fifty-seven when she died. It was an exit too early. I didn't get the time to be with my mother to my heart's content. It was as if a gentle wind had stopped suddenly.

Mother never discussed business matters with us. Never once had she asked us for details of our income. It mattered little to her whether we made a profit or suffered a loss. Instead, she served us with love, day in and day out. She was the epitome of love and affection. I can feel that warmth in my heart even now.

After my mother's death, I handed our ancestral house to my fourth brother and moved to another house.

Each of my brothers manages his own textile showroom. T.S. Anantharaman looks after Kalyan Vastralaya. While T.S. Pattabhiraman manages Kalyan Silks, T.S. Balaraman is in charge of Kalyan Dresses. T.S. Ramachandran is at the helm of Kalyan Sarees.

6

The Story of a Failure

Life is not about success alone. Failures can happen to anyone at any time. A majority of them will be of our own doing. In my life too, there is such a chapter—something I brought upon myself after plunging headlong into something I did not know about.

I've already said I was very interested in acting and movies. My father and I used to watch movies regularly. Thus arose my interest in the tinsel world and the actor in me keenly observed every movie.

Most of the stalwarts of Malayalam cinema were our family friends. G. Venkiteswaran, owner of G.V. Films, Tamil film producer Ratnam Iyer, Mohan of Shogun Films (GoodKnight Mohan), to name a few, were all very close to our family. We used to go on frequent trips with them. Mohan is my father's sister's son. We were together in school and college. Our common interest in movies was one factor that strengthened our bond. We used to go together to watch the new releases. Discussions about the story and acting would go on for days together.

Once on a trip to Sabarimala, the conversation of our friends centred on movies. I shared my passion for movies with G. Venkiteswaran and Ratnam Iyer. They encouraged me when I said I wanted to do something in the field. Film production is a lucrative area, they said, rekindling my passion. I knew acting wasn't an easy affair. So, I tried my hand at film production.

The year was 1982. There was a youth association in Thrissur comprising Balakrishnan of the daily *Express*, my relative and auditor Balaraman, and Raju, who supplied elephant paraphernalia for the annual Thrissur Pooram festival. We would meet up on certain evenings. What bound us all together was our common interest in games and the field of art.

Movies found a place in our discussions during our evening meetings. It was during one such evening meeting that I decided to take up film production. Call it the immaturity of youth or the habit of acting on impulse.

Each one would bring in Rs 1 lakh. That was the decision. And so was born the banner of Ambal Films.

My father was against the idea when I introduced it at home. He warned me against going into unfamiliar areas. He advised me not to go after movies by sidelining our business.

It was tough to convince my father. I told him I needed only Rs 1 lakh. After several rounds of talks, he finally changed his mind. It was a one-time nod. But he was firm on two conditions: One, it must be the first and the last venture. No more movie projects, even if this became a success. Two, the shooting of the film must not be at the cost of one's business. 'Invest money if you must. But back off after that. Let your friends look after the rest,' was what he said.

I agreed. That's how I became a part of Ambal Films. Our first project was a movie based on Perumbadavam Sreedharan's *Ashtapadi*. Sreedharan wrote the screenplay for the movie directed by Ambili. The cast included Bharat Gopi, Devan, Adoor Bhasi, Menaka and Sukumari, among others.

The lyrically beautiful songs, penned by P. Bhaskaran and Vidyadharan Master, were the highlight of *Ashtapadi*. '*Vinninte Virimaaril*', rendered by Yesudas, was the best of the lot. '*Chandana*

Charchitha' by Kavalam Sreekumar and *'Pandu Pandoru Kalath'* by Sujatha captured the hearts of many a listener.

The film was a failure in the theatres despite the presence of a good story and songs. The reason? *Ashtapadi* was released along with three popular films! The movie had to compete with Padmarajan's *Koodevide*, Mohanlal-starrer *Enginei Nee Marakkum* and every family's heart-throb Baby Shalini's *Ente Mamattikuttiyammakku*. While people flocked to watch these movies, our film fell by the wayside.

There was another reason why the film failed to catch the imagination of the people. It was released only in the small theatres of small towns. It was the distributor's failure. Distributors in those days used to take an advance amount from the theatre owners. In the mad rush to secure the advance amount, our distributor approached only the owners of small theatres! So, we got no theatres in the best centres.

So, it was no surprise that the film was a box office disaster. With that, Ambal Films became neck-deep in debt. To tide over the crisis, there was no other solution but to shell out more money. For at stake was the reputation of our family and business. To clear the debts, we gave Rs 10 lakh. The others chipped in with the rest of the amount. Debt-free, we heaved a sigh of relief. And so ended a bitter chapter in our life.

That failure, even to this day, stands as a warning to all who tread the unfamiliar path heeding someone else's words. It was the most valuable lesson I learnt from the world of movies. If you don't look before you leap, you will fall flat on your face.

Another lesson I learnt was to be very shrewd while investing money. We erred in film distribution. The reason? We had no experience in the field. This is where homework comes into play.

Homework is highly essential in anything that one does. We plunged into film-making, doing no homework. We ought to have studied the pre- and post-production scenario, matters to be taken care of, and the pitfalls and measures to be taken in the event of such a crisis. We ought to have done proper homework before entering the film-making field. We never did that. Which is why we badly burnt our fingers.

But I have no regrets. Certain failures are the stepping stones to success.

7

Self-Confidence

'Why don't you diversify?' That suggestion from our very own customers triggered a thought process. Yes, why stick to textiles alone? For weddings, shopping for clothes and gold goes hand in hand. 'You already have a textile shop, Swami. So, why don't you open a shop for gold ornaments too?' asked some of our regular customers. 'It would make shopping easy for us. For we need to come to just one shop for clothes and gold,' they said. That was in 1992.

Initially, we took the suggestion only lightly. But, as days progressed, we gave it a second thought. Not seriously, though. Not a bad idea was what we thought. The truth dawned on us one day. Don't people have an affinity towards gold? Many even hold it close to their heart. That was the beginning of a serious thought process.

We had burnt our fingers badly in the movie business. We couldn't let that happen to the gold business. It would be like playing with fire. If the financial loss in movies was to the tune of Rs 10 lakh, it would be an astronomical sum when dealing with the yellow metal. We would be finished. And so we thought about it not once, but many times over. The textile business runs in the family. We had been doing it for years together. It was not the case with gold. Our forefathers weren't even remotely connected with gold. So, we had to be very careful.

The clamour to begin the jewellery business grew louder day by day. 'Swami . . . when are you beginning the jewellery business? Begin it soon, Swami . . .' We were swarmed with such suggestions day in and day out. The constant queries were our source of inspiration. It was at that time, that I discovered the true meaning of the word 'self-confidence'. The confidence that whatever the situation, the people are with us was something that went beyond words. I firmly believed in two things: One, that Lord Rama will be with us. Two, the people will be with us. We weighed the two on a scale and found them to be of equal measure. 'Do your part, leave the rest to God,' goes the saying. There was no more hesitation. We decided to step into the world of the most precious metal—gold.

I sought the opinion of my wife and children before taking the plunge. Though the children were students, I wanted to know their views too. For I didn't want to be blamed later for not listening to them too. And, in case something happened, I didn't want them to say, 'Father, you could have asked us our opinion too.'

'Do you have to set out on such an adventure?' was what my father asked when I told him my plan. Father was growing old. He was concerned about his children. So, it was only natural that his ageing mind thought this way. Yet, when I explained everything to him, he gave his consent. My brothers too agreed to the plan. It was the most decisive moment of my life.

I don't look back once I've taken a decision. It had been so since my childhood. So, with firm steps, I went forward. As a first step, I decided to thoroughly study the A-Z of the gold business. For this, I went to all the major jewellery shops in Chennai and Kerala. In Kerala, a majority of the shops were in Thiruvananthapuram, Alappuzha, Kottayam, Ernakulam and Kozhikode.

No one ever asked me what the 'textile man' had to do with the jewellery business. I was warmly welcomed wherever I introduced myself. For by then, the fame of the textile brand Kalyan had spread far and wide in Kerala. Everyone encouraged me when I stated the purpose of my visit. The proprietors of all the jewellery shops I went to shared their experiences with me and offered me valuable advice on the dos and don'ts of the business.

I went to all the major jewellery shops in Madras. They were all doing well. One drawback I found was that the shops were tiny. If in Kerala it was less than 500 sq. ft, in Tamil Nadu it was 700–800. I didn't find a single shop with a greater area than this.

Since the shops were small, there were only a few designs. A marriage party was shown hardly four or five designs. If they liked the design, ornaments would be made and handed over to them after one or one and a half months. This was the practice in those days.

It was here that I found a golden opportunity. Our shop would have a lot of varied designs, ample space for customers to try out the ornaments and on-the-spot sales. It would be a one-of-its-kind store in Kerala.

I was doing a makeover of the traditional gold jewellery business. It was something none had dared to do. For it was fraught with great risk.

But I was determined. If I was entering the gold jewellery business, this would be it. I couldn't possibly move out of Thrissur. Our entire roots were in that place. Moreover, my father wouldn't approve of any place other than Thrissur.

And so I began scouting for a big shop in Thrissur. By God's grace, I came across one such building owned by the Devaswom near the Paramekkavu Devi Temple. It was earlier occupied by Hotel Triveni. It had an area of 4200 sq. ft.

The Devaswom wanted me to place a tender. I prayed fervently to Devi Ma. 'Devi . . . we have desired this space. Please grant it to us.' Praying thus, I put a handsome amount into the hundi and placed the tender. God was with us here, too. I won the tender.

As work on the building progressed, the challenges came one by one. There were objections from all quarters. It was not a blockade as such but an effort to dissuade me from the move. I was on good terms with all the jewellery owners in Thrissur. On some days, we had get-togethers to have friendly chats. 'Are you crazy? This is not at all workable. Do you think it's as easy as your textile business? Such a huge building! If you don't know what you are doing, don't do it. You are only inviting trouble . . .' was what all of them said.

They did not say so out of jealousy. Rather, it was a warning out of sheer concern and love for me. The reason? I had earlier said that the entire jewellery sector saw my new endeavour as a huge, risky affair. Some even went to the extent of saying I would shut shop within a year!

My greatest defence amid all this criticism was self-confidence. I merely nodded my head whenever anyone said something. And I did what I pleased.

I got a wealth of support from all those who came to see me while the work on the building was going on. Most of them were our regular customers at the textile shop. 'Swami, it's good that you finally decided to open a jewellery shop. You've heeded our words. We will be with you,' they said.

They praised me for having such extensive space in the jewellery shop. 'A great idea. Hope you will have a lot of designs. Now, we can select all that we like from here. We don't have to wait endlessly to get ornaments made according to our specifications . . .' so went the comments.

Our greatest strength had always been support from the people. We reposed our faith in them. It's the people who kindled the fire of self-confidence in us.

Some jewellers were critical of the place I chose to set up my shop. 'Will anyone ever set up a shop on Swaraj Round? Will anyone come to such a place?' they asked. 'You ought to have opened the shop either on MO Road or High Road,' was the advice they gave me.

But my priority was a parking area for our customers. This is despite the fact there were very few vehicles in those days. But one had to foresee the multiplying of vehicles and the congestion on the roads.

I got the ability to foresee things from my forefathers. 'Think ahead of the times before setting out to do something. It isn't enough to think about today. One has to think of what will happen several years from now,' my grandfather and father used to say. There wasn't an inch of space for parking on MO Road in those days.

When my children scout for a place to set up a shop, the first thing I tell them is to find one with ample parking space. Vehicles rule the present world, I tell them. People will not come to a place where they can't park their vehicles. This is precisely the reason a piece of land on the roadside costs a fortune and why people look for a suitable place to park their vehicles even under the ground!

I spent Rs 75 lakh. I had Rs 25 lakh with me. I took a loan from the Federal Bank for the rest of the amount. According to the practice in those days, jewellery manufacturers from Mumbai used to come with a bag containing ornaments. One didn't have to make a lump-sum, on-the-spot payment. Rather, the money needed to be paid only within a month.

The jewellery manufacturers came looking for us as soon as we advertised the opening of our shop. They gave us a lot of designs on credit. And so, with an investment of Rs 75 lakh, we were all set to open the doors of Kalyan's first jewellery shop. We had the backing of all those who supported our new venture by saying 'We are with you' rather than those who dissuaded us from moving forward. That gave us immense self-confidence.

8

Heart of Gold

8 April 1993. The day the world came to know of a brand name: Kalyan Jewellers. Later, many people asked me whether I could sleep the previous night. To be very frank, I wasn't tense or anxious. But I was very eager to know how the people would respond to our new venture.

I went to sleep as usual. As the inauguration was in the morning, I had to wake up slightly earlier than usual. After practising yoga, I had my bath, said my prayers, ate my food and went to the office.

Murali and Geetha, popular film stars of those days, inaugurated the shop. They came to Thrissur straight from their shooting location in Kozhikode. The designs and trends that Kalyan brought into the jewellery scene began with these two stars.

It was my idea to bring in film stars to inaugurate the shop. For I was very interested in the marketing field. From a young age, I was interested in the life history and marketing techniques of industrial giants. I used to go in search of their books and read them from cover to cover. In them, I scouted for ways to attract customers to one's business.

The inaugural day rush was unprecedented—something even we never expected. There is not even an iota of exaggeration in this. The price of a gram of gold was only Rs 382!

The first sale was to Sri Ramaswamy Temple. The second was to Dr N.V. Ramani, my wife's brother. It's a practice we follow even to this day. Whenever a Kalyan Jewellers showroom is inaugurated anywhere in the world, the first sale always goes to Sri Ramaswamy Temple and the second to Dr Ramani. The first person among the public to buy gold from our shop was a sixty-year-old lady, named Omana, a regular customer at our textile shop.

On learning about our new venture, Omana came to our jewellery shop with her son on the inaugural day around 8.30 a.m. The shop was inaugurated at 9.30 a.m. Omana, the third in line and the first among our customers, bought a gold coin and went home happily. She was the first link in our global chain of customers, which increases with every passing day.

I don't know even to this day why there was such a huge rush of customers on the inaugural day. Maybe it was because of the Malayali's craze for the yellow metal. Or it may have been because of our mind-boggling collection of jewellery. The people till then had no other option but to choose from the small shops they frequented. So, when they spotted a treasure chest of wonders, they flocked to our shop. I think this could have been the reason for the unprecedented crowd.

The main attraction of our showroom was its sheer size. Compared to the sizes of other showrooms, it was enormous. To the people of Thrissur, it was akin to viewing the Thrissur Pooram or smaller poorams. Many people flocked to the place only to have a glimpse of the huge showroom—much like going around a caparisoned elephant and feasting their eyes on its size and beauty!

Kalyan, on that day, marked the beginning of a revolution in the gold market. We were the first to employ women in the sales section.

The controversy over the enormous size of our showroom refused to die down even days after its inauguration. The words of some seemed like a warning. 'Swami, what's built is built. Just because it has been built, it doesn't mean you have to occupy the entire space. Have your jewellery section in the front portion. Do something else with the rest of the building. We don't think having a jewellery showroom in the entire building is workable.' I merely smiled.

A question I had to face many times over was whether I faced any difficulty while diversifying into the gold business from the textile sector. I felt nothing strange while dealing with the yellow metal. As far as purchases are concerned, it's the same in both businesses. Kalyan Jewellers was the first to go to Mumbai and purchase the materials.

Between the two, it could be said there was a greater element of risk in the gold business and the chances of suffering a loss. For, if one wasn't vigilant enough, one could lose heavily as there was the possibility of gold being stolen. It was easy to steal and tuck a pair of studs or a necklace into one's clothes than steal clothes from a textile shop.

During the initial years, we lost some jewellery. This made us vigilant. We soon set up CCTV cameras for surveillance. It was the first of its kind. No one had ever thought of setting up such cameras in jewellery shops. We appointed a person solely to monitor the cameras. Pretty soon, two robbers fell into our net. The news spread like wildfire. There were no more thefts.

One day, it occurred to us there was every possibility of employees themselves replacing the ornaments. What if they replaced a 22-carat piece of jewellery with an inferior quality piece from somewhere else? Our reputation would certainly be at stake if such a thing happened. So, we devised a plan to handle such a situation.

We made the bar code compulsory for all gold ornaments. The practice of linking it to the computers had not yet begun. But we carried out inspections using card readers. It was simply impossible to change the bar code of one and put it for another.

We can say with pride it was Kalyan Jewellers who first brought technology into the gold business in Kerala. Yet another trendsetter was the reform Kalyan brought about in making charges. When Kalyan opened its first shop, the making charges paid by our customers were based on volume (per gram), whereas what we paid our goldsmiths was based on value. At that time, gold prices were more or less stable and this was not cause for concern.

Later, when gold prices started increasing steadily, this practice caused us a huge loss. We revamped the system and started charging the customers making charges as a percentage of the value of gold. As we changed to the percentage system, other jewellery shop owners too followed suit. As in any business, what rivals do, matters!

My children, Rajesh and Ramesh, students of Kerala Varma College, used to come to the shop on holidays and whenever there was a strike in the college. It was history repeating itself. I used to go to our textile shop while in Class VII. What my father taught me, I taught them too. Customers are our greatest strength. Know their likes and dislikes, and act accordingly. This was the gist of what I taught them.

We suffered a setback in the first two months because of the theft of ornaments. There was a slight dip in our profit. Six months into the business, everything stabilized, and we began going steady. I turned my attention to purchasing too. Soon after the inauguration of our shop came Onam. There was a huge rush—just as in our textile shop. My children and I turned into salesmen!

Our greatest wealth was our honest workforce. We could repose faith in 95 per cent of our employees. Their services are indeed laudable. But there were exceptions. Don't we say that all five fingers of our hand aren't the same? As elsewhere, here too we had some dead wood. They left in time. Our very first employees are still with us. Most of them are now general managers.

A change came over me in the initial years. I sprouted wings! My two wings were my two sons. It was through them that Kalyan Jewellers and I flew. I consider myself lucky to have got two sons who could read their father's mind. They could imbibe whatever I said or did. It was so from the time they entered the business.

Rajesh and Ramesh came to the shop only after completing their studies at Kerala Varma College. I left them to themselves to follow their heart's desire. Let them study as much as they wanted for as long as they wanted. 'Studies come first, business later,' I told them.

Rajesh completed his BCom and got his MBA after which he devoted his entire time to business. Ramesh came to the shop after his MCom. Finally, I had someone to share my burden with. With their arrival, I had to shoulder only one-third of the responsibilities. I thank God that I can say with pride I am the father of two responsible children. They spoilt nothing. Rather, they helped our business grow by leaps and bounds.

By God's grace and with the support of the people, within a year, Kalyan Jewellers could be at the forefront of all the leading jewellers in Kerala. We had everything going for us: a jam-packed showroom and roaring business. On some days, work was so hectic that we never got enough time to show all our designs to those who took ornaments for weddings.

Though jewellery makers gave us a month to make the payment, we paid them within fifteen to twenty days. Pleased, they gave us more and more designs. Our stock increased. Soon, we expanded our showroom.

Inventory tallying in the textile business differs from that in the gold trade. In the textile business, one needed to tally the inventory only once a month. Not so in the jewellery business. Here, it needs to be done daily. We tallied the inventory at night after transacting the day's business and downing the shutters.

And so, the year 1993 became the most important page in my Book of Life. More fruitful chapters followed when that page of peace and success turned.

9

Conquering New Skies

I slowly withdrew from the textile business when my presence was constantly required in the jewellery showroom. While comparing the two, I felt that the jewellery business needed greater attention, as I was a new entrant in this line of business. So, I left the textile business to a close relative whom I could trust. Not that I was abandoning it altogether. Rather, I was sidestepping the textile business for another by entrusting it to trustworthy hands. Whenever I got time, I went to the textile shop to inquire about the business.

How can I forget the textile shop altogether? Didn't I begin my business journey there? So, I go there even to this day and spend precious moments there. It's like a return to one's memories and roots.

Not all days are sunny. You have bad days too. Old-timers would say it's the 'evil eye'. I don't know whether there's any truth in it. Certain things in this world are beyond our comprehension. There may not be any scientific basis for it. Yet, when something bad happens when the going is good, people blame it on the 'evil eye'.

You may wonder why I'm saying all this. It's because of an accident that occurred in 1995—two years after we began our jewellery business.

It was a providential escape from the jaws of death. Thanks to God, I didn't have to be hospitalized even for a day!

I was travelling in our Maruti 800. The accident occurred a day after the *kumbhabhishekam* ritual at Sri Ramaswamy Temple. The time was nearing 5 p.m. I was coming from Chembukkavu to the Indoor Stadium. A private bus coming from one of the bylanes rammed our car bang in the middle. Buses are not permitted to enter that lane. However, this one threw all caution to the wind.

I was trapped in the car. I wouldn't have blamed anyone who thought the occupant of the car was dead. Such was the impact of the accident. News of the accident spread far and wide. Many gave me up for dead. I fainted as soon as the accident occurred—one of the reasons everyone thought I wasn't alive.

I was taken straight to Ashwini Hospital. After an hour, I regained consciousness. They took me to Elite Hospital for a detailed check-up. Scanning and many tests were done. Luckily, nothing serious had happened except for a small bruise near the ribs. And so the man who was rumoured to be dead left the hospital that night!

That accident led to serious thought. A change of car. We bought a car that would offer us greater safety in times of accidents like this. I was the only one in the car when the accident occurred. What if the entire family had been in the car? I decided to get a vehicle that offered greater safety assurance and ended up buying a Benz in 1996.

* * *

I have no qualms in saying that our first showroom was a runaway success. We owe it all to the blessings of Lord Sri Rama and our dear customers. Though business was hectic, we never thought of opening a second showroom—until Rajesh finished his studies and came to the shop.

It was grandfather's practice to set up a shop for each one of his children when they grew up. Likewise, the father in me handed over the first shop to Rajesh and began another one for Ramesh. I could be free once each son had his shop to look after. This was all I had in my mind. (Even as I share this with you, an advertisement on my table reads: 'Trust spreads its wings . . . Opening 10 more showrooms in India!' With the opening of these, the total number of Kalyan Jewellers showrooms in the world goes up to 137. By the time this book reaches your hands, the number would have gone up again. We are now aiming to expand further across geographies.)

Many people used to come from Palakkad to our shop in Thrissur. Thrissur had a lot in common with Palakkad. The tastes of the people were more or less the same; though, in Palakkad, the Tamil style was prevalent. But while selecting clothes and jewellery, the tastes of the people from both places were sort of similar.

'Why don't you open a branch in our place too?' It was a question many of those who came from Palakkad asked us frequently. It meant only one thing—that the people of Palakkad were ready to receive us with open arms. That's how we decided to have our second shop in Palakkad.

There was another reason, too, for our decision. My wife, Rama Devi, wanted the children to come back home every night. She wouldn't sleep without seeing her children. All that Rama wanted when we thought of starting a shop for Ramesh was that it should not be too far away—so that he could come home every day. Palakkad was close by. Only, the journey was tedious.

We constructed a building on 40 cents of land on G.B. Road. It was there we started our second shop on 9 April 2000. You may wonder why it took nearly eight years after the first shop to have the second one. The runaway success of our first showroom did not make us overenthusiastic. We never thought of expanding our business and increasing our profits. We only wanted to manage the one that we had to the best of our ability. We were satisfied with the returns from it. That was all we had on our minds. My grandfather's words not to think of profit while doing business were firmly entrenched in our minds. It was our traditional thinking, a shop for each son, that made us change our decision.

Our showroom in Palakkad also did roaring business. Rajesh and I used to go to Palakkad to assist Ramesh in the business. Ramesh had a tough time as he had to drive back to Thrissur from Palakkad in the night after winding up the business for the day. He would reach home past 11 p.m. only to leave for Palakkad early the next morning. However, he felt no strain. He was doing it for his mother. The children were ready to undertake any sacrifice to make her happy. Ramesh enjoyed the long drive even during odd hours. Ramesh said the stress and strain of driving disappeared the very moment he thought about his mother, who stayed awake at night to meet her son coming home after a hard day's work.

There was a great demand for specific designs in both showrooms. The most-sought-after ones were Palakkamala, Kashumala, Nagapadathali, Muthumala and Mullamottumala. The people in both districts gave great importance to tradition. It was only natural that those who lived in traditional houses came to our showroom looking for the ornaments kept in the jewellery boxes of yore. We discovered that there was another kind of consumer in Palakkad. It took us some time to understand this section. I have explained this in one of the subsequent chapters.

I used to select the designs to be displayed in our showroom. In the earlier days, I accompanied our manager Sunny to Mumbai to purchase the ornaments. While jewellery owners here depended on others to purchase and bring bagfuls of ornaments, we went directly to Mumbai to make our purchases. When my children entered the business, they too joined us in making purchases.

While selecting designs, one has to attach great value to the opinions of customers. Most often, what they say will be right. I followed this principle right from the very beginning. As in the textile shop, instead of sitting at the cash counter, I moved around, meeting all our customers. I chatted with them. I gave a patient ear to all their opinions—just as my father and my uncles had taught me from childhood. 'Swami . . . these designs are not up to the mark . . .' 'Swami . . . these designs won't sell . . .' our customers would say. Most of the time, they were right.

There was no compromise on the finish of the items. I was adamant that even if I had to shell out more for the jewellery, I wouldn't compromise on the finish. I was determined not to take orders from people who compromised on the finish of the ornaments.

When we opened our first shop in 1993, the first doubt that crossed our mind was regarding the purity of gold. How could we find out whether the gold we had kept for sale was pure or not? If it wasn't pure, wouldn't it be tantamount to cheating the people? All these questions troubled me since I was relatively new to the field. The fact is, we did not know how to find out the purity of gold.

The only way out was to melt the gold and find its purity. For this, we took a sample ornament from the supplier and melted it into a bar. We lost the manufacturing charges. Never mind. What mattered most was the purity of the metal. We placed the ornaments on the melting machine and found out their purity.

It wasn't enough to convince ourselves of the purity of the metal. Our customers, too, had to be convinced of the purity of the ornaments that they bought from us. The carat analyser machine was new to the market. We bought one and kept it in our first showroom. With that, all who came to our shop to purchase gold could test its purity.

But even machines can go wrong. While racking our brains hard for a solution, we came across BIS in 1995. Isn't the certification by a government body like the Bureau of Indian Standards a recognition of the purity of products? We made the BIS certification mark mandatory for all our ornaments. Here, too, Kalyan Jewellers was a pioneer of sorts!

Trust—it is this simple word that sustains us. It means the world to us.

10

Experience, the Best Teacher

Initially, after Thrissur, most of our customers came from Malappuram. The people of Malappuram had always held gold close to their hearts. Wearing gold and revelling in it were akin to the joy of adorning their hands and feet with mehndi. The rush of people from Malappuram to our showroom in Thrissur made us think of opening a shop in Malappuram. My two sons could manage our two shops and I the third.

Strangely, things don't always turn out as planned. We are all strung together on an invisible thread, the ends of which are in someone else's hands. We are under the control of that awesome power. Whether we like it or not, we cannot but move in whichever direction the string is pulled.

I call that awesome power 'God'. All that has happened, is happening and will happen is determined by God. I don't make any calculations. I just stand there like God's puppet on a string. I move according to His fingers. With His blessings, everything happens for good. I prostrate before Him.

From the idea of two shops for each of my sons, it was God Himself who led us to open the third one. Moreover, we enjoyed the love and trust of our customers. Along with our faith in God, it was the belief that our customers are with us that made us think we would not fail at anything at any cost.

We considered several options before opting for Perinthalmanna as the apt place to open our third shop. On 4 May 2001, we opened Kalyan's third shop at Perinthalmanna. The shop was opened by none other than Mammootty. It was the beginning of a new relationship (I've narrated this in great detail in Chapter 15).

Our business in Perinthalmanna gave us new insights. Having gauged the mindset of the people, we could increasingly offer them designs of their choice. With that, we could keep our customers satisfied and happy.

* * *

Today, I'm narrating my story to you while standing on the brink of my seventy-fourth year. In all these years, the distances that I've covered, the milestones on the roadside, the shady haunts, those who've walked beside me, and those who've gone before me are all here in my heart as different layers in my life. All these together form my experiences and each of these put together, makes us the person we are.

Ogilvy & Mather, one of the agencies that now handles the advertisements of Kalyan, is one of the best advertising agencies in the world. Piyush Pandey, O&M's brain in India, can rightly be called the Acharya of Indian Advertising. Most of the celebrated advertisements have come from the brain of this gentle soul who resembles an army major.

I first met Piyush at the talks preceding the handing over of Kalyan Jewellers' advertisements to O&M. Each word conveyed an idea. There was an element of humour in them. And, like the pearl in the oyster, there was stuff in it.

I wanted to know more about this wonderful man. That's how I began to read *Pandeymonium*, an autobiography of sorts. After the

Foreword, on the first page, marked #1, Piyush wrote: 'Everyone and everything around you is a teacher.'

My reading and my thoughts remained stuck on that one sentence for a long time. It is when the 'around' that Piyush mentioned clings to us that we call it an 'experience'. That experience is our best teacher. We renew ourselves when we learn new lessons. The person you knew yesterday will not be the person you know after an experience.

An experience does not change you physically. Rather, it alters your way of thinking. This is what the great philosopher Jiddu Krishnamurti says about experience and thoughts:

> Thinking is memory, experience, knowledge; memory, stored up in the brain. Knowledge comes from experience. Humanity has had thousands of experiences. Among them is factual, superstitious and hallucinatory knowledge, which is stored as memory in the brain. So, when you ask a question, the result is a thought. Now, that's a fact. We have discussed this subject with several scientists. Some agree; some disagree. This is something which you can find out for yourselves. You have an experience. You think about it. It becomes knowledge. That knowledge which encompasses memory triggers a thought process. You can never think if you don't have experience, knowledge or memory. Hence, through experience and memory, you have knowledge; and thoughts as a reaction to a challenge. We live because of these thoughts . . .

I would like to say from my experience how thoughts and actions gained through experience can make one a better person. My experience is helping me to recreate myself.

How many experiences in seventy years! Even though all those experiences have not been etched in my memory some may not fade away.

A merchant may have more life experiences than a teacher, an artist, a workshop mechanic, a driver or an employee of a company. The reason? A teacher's experiences are confined to the school, just as a driver's experiences are confined to a vehicle. Each one has his or her life surroundings. Yet, all of them, in one way or the other, come into contact with the merchant. For he is the one who interacts most with society. People swarm to him like honeybees to buy the wares he has spread out. So, he meets many people. Through them, he has varied experiences.

In the next chapter, I'll be sharing with you some experiences that are firmly etched in my mind over the last seventy years. There's nothing special about them. Neither are they randomly selected. There's no criterion. I'm not claiming them to be intense either. Something I can recollect from memory as part of my simple life. That's all.

There may have been bigger things. Hiding from the layers of my memory. Remaining elusive.

As I said earlier, these are not mere experiences. These are my teachers. They taught me many things—things that I shall never forget. Which is why they come easily to me.

11

Mind, Take Heed

It had been six months since we opened our first shop. One day, there wasn't much of a crowd. The atmosphere was peaceful. A wedding group was in the showroom. Besides them, there were three or four people. The time was nearing noon.

We used to serve soft drinks to all our customers. We had employed a couple of persons solely for this purpose. On that day, one of our employees served soft drinks to the wedding group too. They had all started drinking it.

Sitting next to the wedding group was a man and his wife who had come to buy a pair of earrings. They had been searching for a suitable pair for a long time. They stared at our employee who was returning after serving soft drinks to the wedding group. I could see all this from a distance. Suddenly, their face lost colour, as if an unnamed emotion was choking them.

I went up to them. 'Swami, what you did now is not correct,' the woman said after staring at me for a while. I was taken aback. 'Why . . . what happened? Is there any problem?' I was upset. It was clear from my shaky voice.

'It was as good as showing partiality. Why do you hold certain people in high esteem?' Saying this, the man looked at the wedding group. They were happily enjoying their drinks.

Suddenly, the truth dawned on me. 'I'm sorry. It was a mistake. I shall soon get you something to drink,' I said with folded hands.

'No, don't bother,' the man said. 'It's not that we wanted something to drink. We won't have it. There's an impropriety in what you did. It's not right to have different parameters for your customers.'

I didn't know what to say. I was at a loss for words. I folded my hands again. There was precious little I could do.

The whole day I sat thinking about what they said. It was as if my mind was caught in a fishhook. It hurt me. That night, after winding up business for the day, I called a meeting of all the employees and narrated what had happened. 'Such an incident should not happen again,' I told them. 'All those who come here are our guests. A person who comes to buy a gram of gold and another who comes to buy a thousand grams are equal before us. There should not be preferential treatment. Everyone should be received and treated with great hospitality. Our attitude towards one and all should be equal . . .'

I couldn't sleep that night. The day's incident brought back memories of another experience—a reason why I was very hurt.

It happened a couple of years before this incident. As the eldest son, it was my duty to look after my mother. She had to be taken to the hospital frequently. Once, she fell on her hands. Though nothing untoward happened, she was in great pain. I took her to the hospital where the doctor recommended an X-ray examination. There were a couple of patients in the room. One hospital staffer seemed to have a soft corner towards some patients at the cost of ignoring the others.

I waited for a long time. My patience was running out. Feeling irritated, I gave him a piece of my mind. It was then he paid attention to us. When my mother's turn came, he took her hands and placed her palms forcefully on the table. 'Oh God . . .' she screamed in pain. It was something I couldn't bear. I was hurt and angry.

'What are you doing?' I screamed at him, unmindful of whoever was in the room. 'Don't you have an iota of conscience? Would you do the same to your mother? You give preferential treatment to some people while considering the rest as your enemies. Are you a human being?'

I gave him quite a mouthful. What made me furious was his partiality towards some people.

This incident came to my mind when the man and his wife who had come to our shop felt irritated at the bias shown to them by one of our employees. Maybe that's what pained me. It brought me memories of my mother. I felt my mother's cries echoing in my mind.

From that day, there never was a word called 'discrimination' in Kalyan Jewellers' dictionary. For us, then and now, all are equal. Be it a person who buys a gram of gold or 1000 grams.

* * *

The second experience was also during the initial days of our jewellery business. One morning, a couple of officials from the Income Tax department came to our shop and began a search operation. They sought several documents, which my staff handed over to them. We had nothing to hide. While the search operation was going on, an officer shouted at one of my staffers. Though taken aback, he calmly replied to the officer's query. Irked, the officer slapped him on the cheek.

I was watching all this. It was as if the officer had slapped me. Did I stroke my cheek? I don't remember. The person who received the blow was not just a staffer to me. He was a member of my family. From the day I first stepped into the shop till this day, I have considered all our staff as members of the family. They are one among us. That's what my grandfather and father taught us. Kalyan is an extended family.

So, if someone slaps my staffer, it is akin to slapping me. I lose my cool if I see injustice. Circumstances or surroundings don't matter when I am angry. What happened next was a repeat of the hospital incident. 'Who are you to slap my staffer?' I screamed at the officer. 'What was his mistake that you had to slap him? Even if he has done something wrong, who gave you the right to slap him?' I asked him.

With that, he turned his ire on me. 'Go ahead, slap me,' I challenged him. 'But don't you dare touch my staff,' I said.

Sensing the scene going out of hand, Income Tax Commissioner Vijayakumar intervened. He was a soft-spoken, gentle person. He knew one of his men had erred. 'Leave it . . . leave it . . . he may have acted on the spur of the moment,' he tried to pacify me.

Though the war of words ended there, I wasn't ready to leave it at that. I scrutinized all documents regarding income tax laws. Not even in one document was it mentioned that the officer who comes to search the premises of anyone has the authority to manhandle members of the staff.

I had taken a petition too, along with the assessment papers, when I went to the Income Tax office. 'Sir, I have a complaint,' I told the commissioner after I had submitted my assessment papers. 'One of your men slapped my staffer on the day you came to search my premises. I want you to take action against him. Here's my complaint,' I said.

The commissioner refused to accept my petition. 'He will lose his job if I forward this complaint. I shall make him apologize to your staffer,' he said.

'I don't want him to lose his job. I am ready to withdraw my complaint if he apologizes to my staffer,' I said.

And so, the officer came to our shop and apologized to the man he had slapped. The incident became a topic of discussion among the staff. It further cemented the ties between us and the employees.

Anyone in the Kalyan family has the freedom to approach me with whatever personal problems he or she has. I have given everyone the freedom to do so. There is no need to wait for permission to speak to me. My doors are always open, and anyone can walk right into my office and speak his or her mind.

We don't hide things from each other either. It is this transparency that is the sign of our success. The word 'Trust' is not confined to our business alone. We hold it close to our hearts in our relationships too.

* * *

The third incident has an element of pathos in it. Sometimes man becomes uncompassionate, especially in times of adversity.

I had earlier said some people brought jewellery for us—Malayalees and non-Malayalees, local goldsmiths and big jewellery makers in Mumbai. They used to come with a big bag full of jewellery.

Once, one of them gave us gold jewellery mixed with copper. He was a local goldsmith. We found out about the foul play and handed him over to the police.

He came from a poor family. His wife came crying to me. 'We have two small children and aged parents to look after. Please help us,' she said. I felt pity for them. I called up the police station and made arrangements to release him.

There are many such experiences. All this came to my mind in the twinkling of an eye. There are many more . . .

12

Lessons from Our Second Showroom

Let me come back to the days of our jewellery business. We had to confront a lot of realities in the market while opening our showroom in Palakkad. It was the gateway to a host of opportunities. That was what led us to Palakkad—the district bordering Kerala and Tamil Nadu

Palakkad was a small town in those days. The place was devoid of swarming crowds and huge concrete structures. The people of Palakkad depended on Thrissur and Coimbatore for anything and everything. Palakkad was like a household that always depended on its neighbourhood.

Coimbatore wasn't strange to them, as any place beyond Walayar had a Tamil flavour. For the people of Palakkad, it was akin to having the same affinity towards a relative's house. The consumers of many shops in Coimbatore were from Palakkad.

The people in the western parts of Palakkad preferred Thrissur to Coimbatore. The Pooram and Vela festivals further cemented their ties with Thrissur. What brought them close to Thrissur were the captivating sights of the majestic elephants and the riveting sounds of the *melam* where they often lost themselves.

Business in Palakkad lost its sheen when the populace split up in two and went to Coimbatore and Thrissur. It was no wonder that Palakkad had only small shops.

While Palakkad thus stood as a satellite town of Coimbatore and Thrissur, an earth-shattering incident occurred—bomb blasts at Coimbatore in 1998. In all, fifty-eight people died in the twelve explosions that occurred within a radius of 12 km at eleven places. Around 200 people were injured. The impact the terrorist attack that shook the nation had on the industrial and economic sectors of Coimbatore wasn't at all insignificant. Post the explosions, Coimbatore gained a risky and uncertain image. People were terrified of going to the place. Soon, the flow of people from Palakkad to Coimbatore ebbed.

The people of Palakkad, who always depended on Coimbatore, began shopping in their hometowns. Palakkad soon became a beehive of commercial activity. This was most clear in the gold jewellery business. All the small shops in the area began buzzing with action.

This sea change had a cascading effect on our showroom in Thrissur. Soon, crowds began thronging our shop too. The people of Palakkad who came to our showroom were literally 'inviting' us to their place. Here began our chapter in Palakkad. We employed the same time-tested business tactics in Palakkad too: a huge showroom with ample car-parking area and vast stocks of material. It was meant to create a gigantic impression on the minds of the people. We needed only one-tenth of the space to showcase ourselves as bigger than the biggest showroom in Palakkad. But we started in a big way. We were certain we could create marvels in that huge showroom.

But we underestimated the people of Palakkad. Folks who came to Thrissur to purchase ornaments were financially very well off and had great expertise in buying and selling. It was not so with the people who went shopping in Coimbatore. Their temperaments were different. The treatment they demanded, customer service, billing, discount—all were entirely different from the people who came to Thrissur. It was something we failed to realize in the beginning.

We changed our strategy when we realized the two different traits of the consumers from the Palakkad region. For around a year, Ramesh concentrated only on our showroom in Palakkad. He stayed in Palakkad for weeks together, gently setting aside his mother's request to come home daily. He constantly interacted with the people. In fact, within a year, Ramesh became a native of Palakkad!

The lessons we imbibed from the Palakkad experiment helped us in no small way in our future endeavours. Though it was our second showroom, the lessons Palakkad taught us come to the fore whenever we open a new showroom. We set out to script history in the lingo we picked up from Palakkad.

'Go as local as you can' was the lesson Palakkad taught us. In marketing terms, it is known as going 'hyper-local'. It means we should fashion our business style according to the likes and dislikes of the locality. Rather than selling what we have on our hands, we must try to understand what the people want and sell that to them. Trying to sell what we have won't work. We must keep a tab on what sells in the market and plan a sales strategy after gauging the mindset of the people. We obtain a winning formula by understanding the market trends and including some of our methods in it.

Know your consumer thoroughly—that's what is needed. Simply put, most Punjabis prefer to have rotis over rice. Whenever we open a new shop, we don't compete with the big names in the business. Rather, we compete with the lesser-known shops in the region. This is the first lesson we learnt from Palakkad. Be hyper-local as much as you can. Be it the staff, stock or campaign—all of it must have a local flavour. We must become one with them.

We went to Palakkad as Thrissur natives. But when we were convinced of many things in Palakkad, we became natives of that region. If we don't have this realization, we will always be outsiders in that area. We must become one among the locals to dispel any feeling of alienation among the customers.

With footprints from Palakkad, we went to Perinthalmanna. It made things easy for us. We only had to implement the lessons we learnt in Palakkad. Soon, we became natives of Perinthalmanna too. With that, Kalyan Jewellers became a name to reckon with.

* * *

I had earlier hinted at certain trends we had introduced in the gold business. Among them were the ways and means to win over the confidence of the customers. Let me elaborate on them.

The gold business was a disorganized sector when we entered the field. It never had a unified structure. Ninety-nine per cent of the business was in the hands of small players who lay scattered here and there. The business practices too were varied. There were only one or two big brands.

Traders, in those days, formulated their strategies exclusively to reap profits. Consumers never mattered to them. How could one do business without giving due consideration to the buyer? We were surprised. We had two options before us. Either be with the small traders and do business in their style, or have our way and bring the disorganized sector under a unified umbrella.

The first option wouldn't work out. For we had our point of view. The consumer was important. So, the only way out was to change the system. That's why we started cleansing the system by making sweeping changes. The carat analyser, BIS certificate and finding out the purity of metal by melting it were all part of that cleansing process.

We were trendsetters. So, it was no wonder that the others had to follow suit. Till then, the small traders were cashing in on the ignorance of the consumer. Maybe they too were ignorant of the right practices. We taught the consumers many things—from how gold is made to testing its purity.

What do traders normally do when they have a chain of shops? They advertise by proclaiming the greatness of their shops. We never did that. Rather, our campaigns were to teach our consumers a thing or two. It was akin to an education programme. Thus, we could create a huge impact on society.

Small traders were forced to toe the line when consumers began questioning them regarding the purity of gold and BIS certification. Traders who sold their stuff according to their whims and fancies at prices of their own choice had to face uncomfortable questions from the customers regarding their pricing. Thus, the gold trade began to have standardized form.

We strived to fill the hearts of the people with Trust. There must be an element of Trust in whatever one does. This is our credo. We conducted a survey on the inauguration of our showroom in Palakkad. 'What's the factor that draws you to Kalyan Jewellers?' was the question. We were eager to know what factor led the people to our showroom— was it the pricing, customer service or the wide range of jewellery? 'We have full faith in Swami,' said 90 per cent of the people.

That's the moment we realized the value of the word that leads us: Trust. The people trust us. They trust what we say. It is not a simple thing. Our next challenge was to cement the trust the people reposed in us. The campaign highlighting the purity of our jewellery was part of that challenge. We had blazed a trail. Seeing the trust the people had in us, other traders had no other option but to follow the same example in their business. The impact it made was tremendous.

13

A Flame Named Desire

We arrived at the word 'Trust' after travelling long distances. Along the way, we encountered many highs and lows. We even saw the mistrust of others. To the people, we were mere textile traders when we arrived in the intrinsic four-letter world of gold in 1993. A group trading in textiles for years together. That was the image we had. The word 'Kalyan' brought only images of a textiles shop to the people. It wasn't easy to wipe out that image from their minds and have a new one in its place. The reason? Those involved in the jewellery business had a tradition of seventy to eighty years. So, it was no wonder the people of Kerala accepted them as traditional jewellers.

The way of thinking was entirely different twenty-five years ago. 'Do they know this trade?' was what many thought when we set out on the golden route. That outlook changed as the years passed.

After Perinthalmanna, our next destination in Kerala was Kollam. Though Thiruvananthapuram and Kozhikode were on our minds, we zeroed in on Kollam as the most suitable place.

The practice in those days was to look for a 'vacuum' while scouting the place to open a showroom. Big brands had already made their presence felt in Thiruvananthapuram and Kozhikode. It was tough to find a space among them. Moreover, we would have had to run at a loss for one or two years. In business parlance, it is called 'bleeding'. There would be nothing left in the cash boxes. We were not in a good financial position then to take on such a huge risk. At the most, we may have been able to hold on for five to six months. By then, the business would have needed to start generating profit.

A market opportunity—without major competitors and a market size that can absorb future competition—this was our yardstick. We were convinced that there was one such place waiting for us—a vacuum.

Had it been now, we wouldn't have thought of a vacuum. Now, we don't open showrooms looking at a vacuum. The reason? We are confident that even if we run at a loss for one or two years, we can make a profit in the following years. There is no harm, even if it bleeds. We can tide over the crisis later.

Take, for example, our experience in the Middle East. When we touched the shore, our main rivals had eighty showrooms. To measure up to them, we had to pump in money till it reached a turnover of Rs 2000 crore. There was no point in expecting profits. Yet, we took the plunge and in three years, we crossed the Rs 2000-turnover mark. We achieved it because we had the capacity and strength to do so. Such was the strength of our brand. It wasn't so in the beginning. Precisely why we stepped into a safe place—Kollam.

From a showroom each for my two sons and one for myself, my dreams soared and crossed all boundaries. I set my sights on expanding our showrooms beyond Kerala.

Tamil Nadu was a perfect choice. Not only because of its fertile business soil but also because it was from Tamil Nadu that our roots began—a place so close to our heritage and tradition. From that state, I selected Coimbatore. The shock and awe of the bomb blasts had by then left Kovai town. Life and trade had started afresh.

From a shop for Rajesh and a second one for Ramesh, I thought of Kerala for Rajesh and Tamil Nadu for Ramesh. That was how in 2003, Kalyan Jewellers opened its fourth showroom in Coimbatore.

* * *

Disputes in family businesses occur because of sibling rivalry or differences of opinion between the father and his children. It's a possibility if both the sons are rooted in one place—another reason behind my plans to open a showroom in Tamil Nadu.

Four years after setting foot in Tamil Nadu came our fifth showroom in Erode. That's a long gap, many of you may think. It's because we were investing in three places.

One, our customers. We have no existence without them. We were engrossed in providing them with what they wanted. Second, research. We were studying the market trends and looking for ways and means to reinvent ourselves scientifically according to them. We did a lot of surveys for this. Third, our employees. We took them into confidence and moved forward. Thus, the assets of the big family called 'Kalyan' increased (not financially, but morally, and in terms of employee strength).

After starting showrooms in the smaller towns of Tamil Nadu, we finally set foot in Chennai. We knew it was impossible to survive in Chennai without a minimum sales turnover of Rs 1000 crore. Everything was expensive. From showrooms to advertisements to placing hoardings, we needed loads of money. There were around five or six famous establishments with plenty of showrooms. To compete with them was war!

It was difficult to get a sales turnover of Rs 1000 crore from just one showroom. We had to open new shops. For that, we needed capital. This is precisely why, even though the fame of Kalyan Jewellers had reached every nook and cranny of Tamil Nadu, we were slow to decide on opening our showroom in Chennai.

It's been five years since we opened Kalyan's showroom in Chennai. We now have a clear-cut plan. How much money we should invest in the market, what's the profit we'd get from it, for how many years should we bleed for it . . . we now have a definite 'route map'—drawn from years of experience.

We never had such a plan in the beginning. We were merely filling the vacuum with the first five or six showrooms after watching the scenario carefully. There wasn't scope for a Plan B.

As I've said earlier, in those days, we collectively did all the jobs. Rajesh, Ramesh and I used to receive the customers, show them the various jewellery designs, bill the items and collect the money. It made us understand the hardships faced by our employees. We learnt through experience their mental and physical fatigue and the time lost by waiting on customers . . . By handling different customers, we could understand their likes and dislikes. Rajesh and Ramesh easily learnt the pulse of the customers—the jewellery each one would like to wear, how to select designs of their choice. To me, it was a big blessing.

Normally, the new generation arrives by outrightly rejecting the values of the older generation. It didn't happen in Kalyan Jewellers. Though Rajesh and Ramesh had their ideas, they never rejected our past. It was a historical document for them. A treasure chest containing a variety of priceless information.

Our confidence level increased by leaps and bounds through the opening of our Kollam showroom. That's how we landed in Thiruvananthapuram. Along with that, we started our second showroom in Thrissur. We learnt newer lessons with the opening of more and more showrooms. All of us understood the value of sweat. Sweating it out, we moved forward. Each drop of sweat that fell to the ground became a foundation stone for the future.

It was the desire that led us forward. That desire took on newer meanings as we took each step forward. A desire is something any human being has. It was to fulfil that desire that we strived so hard.

More than that, with the opening of more and more showrooms, our Kalyan family was expanding. Fresh staff joined our workforce. Their families too became part of our family. And so, Kalyan Jewellers became the reason for bringing joy into many lives.

It is said desire is the cause of unhappiness. But here, I'd like to follow the words of Sadhguru: 'Without desire, there is no universe. In the absence of desire, there is no wind, no waves, no sunrise, not even the vibration of atoms. There is no body, no throbbing of life, even the breath will fail. The universe has not said you shouldn't have desires. There is no greater foolishness than thinking everything will be all right if you abandon desires.' This is what Sadhguru says in one of his books.

It is desire that makes each cell in the body perform. When a disease-causing virus enters your body as an uninvited guest, no single cell takes pity on it thinking 'Poor fellow, let it too survive' and waits for your permission. The very moment a virus enters your body, the cells arm themselves and begin a combined attack. This is because Nature has given each cell the desire to live. Therefore, it will withstand any hardship and put up a brave fight to defend its desire to live.

How big can your desires be? Sadhguru has answers to this too. 'You already have desires. So, why be stingy with them? Be as large-hearted as you can be. If you don't dare to dream big and are going to shackle your desires in a confined room, how will you be able to tackle bigger things in life?'

It's a question I have asked myself many times: If you place your desires (projects, in business terms) in a square box, how will you have the mental and physical strength to move forward?

We started with the desire to open a single shop. From one, we branched out to two and later, spread to the entire state and Tamil Nadu. From a small desire, we have now moved to the international scene.

What kindled my passion was the flames of desire. Along with them was the feeling of contentment that came from the prayers, happiness and blessings of thousands of families. It was the same flame of desire that was in the hearts of all those who toiled hard from the inception of Kalyan Jewellers. It was precisely this flame that led us unflinchingly towards our desired goal.

14

Starry Vigil

Kalyan's label as a textile shop slowly faded after the opening of our Palakkad showroom. In its place, we gained the image of newcomers who brought in many changes in the jewellery business. It was at this stage that we began expanding our social circle and many entered the portals of the Kalyan family. Our story will not be complete without saying a few words about them. The reason? They were with us when we climbed the steps of success. They held our hands as we attained great heights. Their handprints are part and parcel of the Kalyan Jewellers' journey.

Among them, Mammootty holds the pride of place. Our association with the great actor began in 2003. We had approached him in connection with the opening of our showroom in Perinthalmanna. Much before this, Mammootty, the man and the actor, had secured a place in our hearts. Whenever *Oru Vadakkan Veeragadha* is aired on TV, I spend at least ten minutes in front of the screen. I hold close to my heart the innumerable characters he has essayed in films over the years.

Maybe because of my latent wish to act in movies, I used to adore every single character Mammootty portrayed on the silver screen. They had a powerful influence on me.

I'm familiar with Mammootty, the actor, through his screen presence. Of Mammootty, the man, I had only hearsay reports. To people who are not familiar with him, he is rumoured to be haughty and proud, a person who always keeps to himself. But those who know him personally will beg to differ. The man you know from the outside is not the man you know from the inside.

In the olden days, jewellery shop advertisements featured only women. To have a man in their place was simply unthinkable. It was during such a time that we brought in Mammootty as our brand ambassador. Here, too, we opted to tread the hitherto untrodden path.

But, before starting out, we put our heads together. Rajesh, Ramesh and all our family members became part of that thinking process. Women have always held gold ornaments close to their hearts. Those who frequent jewellery shops too are women.

The ties between women and jewellery are inseparable—the reason why jewellery ads featured only women. Changing the trend is adventurous and risky too. But we took the plunge. There had to be a change in the style of advertising too.

Bearing this in mind, we approached Mammootty after the inauguration of our showroom in Perinthalmanna. Mammootty had a very strong fan base in Malappuram. So, we struggled to think of another personality to inaugurate our showroom in place of the great actor.

We met Mammootty at the shooting location of the movie *Pattalam* in Palakkad. The love and adoration we had for the great actor were beyond words. From the warm welcome we received, it was evident he, too, held us in great esteem. He had a great understanding of our business in the world of yellow metal. Mammootty was well-informed on any topic, be it technology or politics. He would be the first person to know about any tech innovations. Such was his interest in the world around him. Even amidst his busy schedules, he would keep abreast of what was happening in the world with inquisitive and wondrous eyes. The apt word to describe his vigilant nature is his movie—*Jaagratha*!

It was no wonder such a well-informed actor like Mammootty knew about our business thoroughly. But he was hesitant when we requested him to be our brand ambassador. 'Do you think so?' he asked. He was doubtful, as his presence might create a kind of strangeness in a world of advertisements dominated by women.

'It is not just our love for Mammootty, the actor, that made us think on these lines,' we told him. 'We need a brand ambassador in Kerala. We can't think of anyone else but you. It's for the first time that a jewellery shop is going to feature a man in its advertisements. We have a plan and a goal to achieve. We intend to tell the people a few things. We believe you are the best to undertake that mission. No other actor can step into your shoes. We need a personality like you who is loved and respected by all. We want someone who doesn't do advertisements for the sake of money—someone with an unblemished image. Considering all this, you are the perfect choice.'

Still, Mammootty wasn't convinced. 'I like you, Swami,' he said. 'To be featured in an advertisement? Well . . . no,' he said.

'It's not just an advertisement that you will do,' we explained further. 'It's social service. Crores of people are being duped every year in the gold jewellery sector. The people will heed your words if you make a statement. This way, at least some people may not fall prey to cheating practices. They will be convinced the person appearing before them in an advertisement is not there to make money but is a flagbearer of efforts aiming at social welfare.'

Finally, Mammootty nodded. He understood the meaning of our words. Thus, Mammootty, the great actor, became not only Kalyan Jewellers' brand ambassador but also the campaigner for a social cause.

For one or two years, Mammootty featured in our advertisements to create awareness among the people. He won the trust of the people by speaking authoritatively on BIS and other matters. We took Mammootty to our labs, where he saw and learnt many things for himself. It was then that he started starring in our advertisements. He wasn't parroting hollow dialogues. Rather, they were from the heart as he joined hands with us in our great endeavour.

Our next aim was to reach out to our customers and give them the same wonder-eyed experience—the one we felt when we first met the great actor. There is an intrinsic radiance in the three-syllabic word 'Mam-moo-tty'. That radiance bowls us over and takes us to the peaks of ecstasy. We wanted our customers, too, to experience it.

We hit upon a plan. Mammootty would make his presence felt on the most joyous occasion of their lives. He would visit the houses of 100 selected customers who had purchased jewellery from Kalyan Jewellers' showrooms, on their wedding day.

We had only three showrooms at that time. 'You may have to travel all over Kerala. It's a strenuous ask,' I told Mammootty.

But Mammootty had his doubts. It is here that we saw the perfectionist in the man. He would decide on any matter only after examining all its aspects. Precisely why we don't see his name in any controversies. He insisted on accuracy and keenness in anything that he did.

'How is it possible? How can I attend a hundred weddings? What if they don't appreciate my presence . . .' This was how Mammootty responded when we approached him with the idea of visiting the houses of our customers on their wedding day.

'Not a single soul will resent your presence. They will not only appreciate it but also consider it a blessing on their most auspicious day. Your presence will stupefy them, making them forget themselves. This is what's going to happen,' we promised him.

Mammootty agreed to the idea. We took him to 100 villages in Kerala. As the news of his visit spread far and wide, a sea of villagers flocked to the houses. The weddings turned out to be a grand festival of sorts. Mammootty chatted with the members of the houses and had food with them. As he bid goodbye to them, many still could not fathom whether it was all for real or a dream.

Our idea had a cascading effect too. Till then, Mammootty was considered one who kept his distance from others, one who kept others at a distance and one who was very haughty. His visit to the houses of our customers on their wedding day changed the false perception in the minds of the people. We take pride because we could present the true Mammootty before the people of Kerala.

It's going to be twenty years since our association with Mammootty. Though not our brand ambassador, the warmth of our friendship has not waned even a wee bit. Despite his busy schedule, he is a constant presence at all our private functions. We too happily accept all his invitations.

Our experience proved that the public perception of Mammootty, the actor, was false. He is a genuine person in every sense of the term—one who has no qualms in speaking his mind or showing his emotions. Be it anger, joy or sorrow . . . Mammootty doesn't know how to hide his feelings.

Mammootty minces no words if he dislikes something—the reason many consider him to be very arrogant. It is not arrogance but the outburst of an untainted human being. Hypocrisy is an alien word to him. An honest and straightforward person, Mammootty is a friend for all seasons to us. We consider his friendship a great asset.

We met Mohanlal during our campaigns with Mammootty. He wasn't a brand ambassador of Kalyan Jewellers. He inaugurated our renovated showrooms.

In 2003, a programme, 'Thiranottam', was organized in Thiruvananthapuram to celebrate twenty-five years of Mohanlal's acting career. The programme was held on the maidan of MG College, Mohanlal's alma mater. We were glad to associate ourselves with the programme. Kalyan Jewellers was the main sponsor of the Thiranottam event. That was when Mohanlal asked the people of Kerala, 'What is a celebration for me without you . . .'

That statement from Mohanlal became an instant hit. We benefitted from it. For Kalyan's esteemed customers too were invitees to the Thiranottam programme. Along with Mohanlal, Malayalees' favourite actor, our brand too shone brightly.

Actor Dileep has also associated with us for seven years. Dileep acted in one of Kalyan's most touching advertisements. The advertisement, where Amitabh Bachchan donned the garb of a schoolteacher and Dileep was his former student, played a great role in taking our trusted brand to greater heights all over the world.

One of our great achievements was our association with various actors and getting them involved in something different. It was not for money or more fame that they associated with us. Rather, it was to express their solidarity with certain ideas that we put forth. They still have love and trust towards us in their hearts. All those who have associated with us even once express their happiness in our growth even though they are no more a part of our brand. They call us up, make inquiries and stand by us whenever we go through a bad patch. We hope they will be with us in the future too.

15

And the Sea Came Along . . .

Our business in Kerala and Tamil Nadu helped in laying a solid financial foundation. That's what made us enter Karnataka. Our confidence level increased after kick-starting business in the markets of Karnataka, including Bengaluru. It didn't matter to us even if it bled for a year after investing Rs 300–400 crore. Our next step was to gain a foothold in Andhra Pradesh.

Kalyan Jewellers scripted history by opening thirteen showrooms in a year in that state. It was the most unthinkable thing for a Kerala brand to do in a vast playground like Andhra Pradesh. Many could not believe their eyes! Who would think we would make such a huge investment in another state! One word suffices to describe such a daring act: Courage. Time had given us the capability to take such an adventurous step.

We implemented in Andhra Pradesh on Day One the experiment that took us a long time in Kerala. We opened showrooms one after another and, along with them, 'My Kalyan' centres. As our brand ambassador, we introduced Nagarjuna, the king of Telugu cinema. Here too, as in other places, we went hyper-local. We sensed the pulse of the people and offered them the jewellery of their choice. We sensitized the people to the universal malpractices in the jewellery sector. Andhra Pradesh was no exception. Thus, we could win the confidence of the people.

It took us nearly one and a half decades to win the confidence and trust of the people of Kerala. But all it took to spread over the entire south India was a few years. Our evolution was like a rivulet trickling down a rocky hilltop to expand into a stream and finally change into a river.

Beyond a point, it is difficult to overflow and spread out in south India. One must then reduce the flow of water. We found there was no scope to open new showrooms. It became impossible to open fresh showrooms every year as we did in the initial years. At the most, we could open one or two. This predicament forced us to look for hitherto unexplored shores.

We had two options before us: either cross the sea and touch the shore of the Middle East. Or flow above the Vindhyas. The latter was a challenging task. This market is entirely different from the south Indian one. It would be the first time a jewellery group from the south made a move outside the region. Each state has a different taste for jewellery. Now, this would require a huge investment. Despite the challenges, we moved to other states.

And so, for the first time, Kalyan Jewellers stepped outside south India and set foot in Gujarat. We knew very well that opening one or two showrooms in that state would not be sufficient. We had to have at least fifty showrooms outside the South, to get a firm grip on our business in that region. The reason?

Our rivals were powerful with seventy to eighty showrooms. To open fifty showrooms, we needed at least three years. For each market differed from the other.

We could open thirteen showrooms in a single year because of the uniform nature of the markets in Andhra Pradesh. Though there were slight differences, they were negligible. But this is not the case outside south India. The nature of the market in Rajasthan is entirely different from that of Gujarat and West Bengal. There would be marked differences between the markets in Maharashtra and Punjab.

So, it would be possible to reach these states only in three to four years. We couldn't start in a small way either, fearing losses. We were competing with giants in the field. The money each one spends on advertising is simply mind-boggling. There was no point in playing the role of a supporting actor. A supporting actor is always a supporting actor. He can never become a superstar. To be a superstar, you had to start as a hero.

You had to have inventory like them and advertise your products like them. In other words, be big like them. Despite all this, there is no guarantee that those in that region would accept a player from the south. To instil confidence in them and win their trust was a challenging task.

We knew that only a person who was widely loved, respected and held in high esteem by the people could introduce a group from the southernmost state to the world beyond. It was this thinking that led us to the doors of the Bachchan family. We were not foolish to think that the doors of the family would open before us easily. Still, we decided to knock on their doors.

As a first step, we prepared a presentation for Amitabh Bachchan. In it, we went from our humble beginnings to our latest projects. We laid stress on our efforts to conscientize the jewellery sector and ways and means to cleanse and purify the system. We also stated why we were extending our invitation to him. 'Through you, we wish to be known all across India. We can think of no one else but you. In all the southern states, we invited their superstars to introduce us to the people. Here, we need someone who is more than a superstar. Rather, a towering personality who towers far above the world of cinema . . . There can be no replacement for Amitabh Bachchan. Should the answer be a "no", we have no intention of seeking the services of another celebrity . . .' We e-mailed our comprehensive presentation to Amitabh Bachchan.

For days together, we waited with our fingers crossed. One day, we got a message from Bachchan sir's office for an audience with him.

The meeting was scheduled at Bachchan sir's office in Juhu. We left for Mumbai. Along with me were my sons Rajesh, Ramesh and our marketing team. Our appointment was scheduled for 3 p.m. We reached Bachchan sir's office ten minutes early. It's my habit to reach any place early enough. I expect the same from others too. But my children had warned me. 'He's a great personality and, hence, may be very busy. He may be late in arriving. You must never be impatient.' I could foresee the situation even if they hadn't told me.

Bachchan sir's office was next to his residence. A minute to three, a man came walking down the path to the office. It was someone we had seen only on the silver screen. A towering personality who, with his over-six-foot figure, made Indian cinema bow before him. A sea which hid the roaring waves in its sounds.

He was none other than Amitabh Bachchan. At exactly 3 p.m., he was on the chair right before us. For the first five minutes, we talked about family matters. From there, he came straight to the point. 'I will speak neither about business nor about remuneration,' was how he began the conversation.

'I must be convinced of the brand I'm associating with. My team has handed the details to me. I've gone through the report. But I must know about you from you.' These were Bachchan sir's words.

I narrated to him our origins. I explained to him what we were doing at present and what we were planning to do. Like a smart school kid, he listened intently to what we said. After a while, he asked: 'Why do you need a person like me? Will an eighteen-year-old girl listen to the words of a seventy-year-old man? She may like my movies, but does that mean she will pay heed to what I say about jewellery? So, you give it a second thought . . .'

'We firmly believe that only you can promote our brand here,' we told him.

As in the movies, he sat silent for a while. Visible was the same stone-faced expression we are so familiar with in his movies. We rambled on about our fight to ensure fair play in the jewellery business.

Scenes from the inauguration of Kalyanram Textiles, which began functioning at the Municipal Stand in Thrissur on 17 May 1972.

Rajesh and Ramesh Kalyanaraman as children.

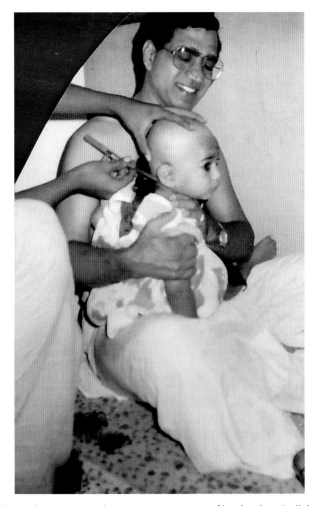

T.S. Kalyanaraman at the tonsuring ceremony of his daughter Radhika.

(Left to right) Ramesh Kalyanaraman, T.S. Kalyanaraman, T.K. Radhika, Ramadevi and
Rajesh Kalyanaraman holidaying in Kodaikanal.

Mohanlal inaugurating the Palakkad showroom of Kalyan Jewellers,
with T.S. Kalyanaraman to his right.

Mammootty inaugurates the second showroom of Kalyan Jewellers in Thrissur on 5 August 2007, with T.S. Kalyanaraman next to him.

C.K. Chandrappan, T.S. Kalyanaraman, chief guest Mammootty, K.P. Rajendran,
Therambil Ramakrishnan and T.S. Anantharaman (Catholic Syrian Bank)
at the centenary celebrations of Brand Kalyan.

(Left to right) Karthik Ramani (MD, Kalyan Developers), Kalyan Jewellers' executive director Rajesh Kalyanaraman, Rishikesh Kalyan, Kalyan Jewellers' executive director Ramesh Kalyanaraman, Nagarjuna, T.S. Kalyanaraman, Amitabh Bachchan, Vikram Prabhu, Prabhu, Shivraj Kumar, Aishwarya Rai and Manju Warrier at the inauguration of Kalyan Jewellers' flagship showroom in Chennai in 2015.

Amitabh Bachchan speaks at the inauguration of Kalyan Jewellers' showroom in Jodhpur, Rajasthan.

Brand Ambassador Katrina Kaif, flanked by Karthik Remani, Ramesh Kalyanaraman, T.S. Kalyanaraman and Rajesh Kalyanaraman, inaugurates the 100th showroom of Kalyan Jewellers in Ranchi on 12 August 2018.

Amitabh Bachchan presents a special award to T.S. Kalyanaraman at the 44th IAA World Congress held in Kochi. The award, bestowed by the International Advertising Association, recognizes the contribution of Kalyanaraman in building Kalyan Jewellers as a global, endearing brand and taking it from a regional brand in Kerala to an international brand.

Deep in conversation at the annual Navaratri Pooja function at the Kalyan residence in Thrissur.

When the stars descended in Thrissur—the Kalyanaraman family's annual Navaratri Pooja function at their Thrissur residence is a star-studded occasion.

The next generation: Executive directors Rajesh and Ramesh Kalyanaraman have been a part of the jewellery business since its inception and are well-positioned to take over this empire.

Ramesh Kalyanaraman, T.S. Kalyanaraman and Rajesh Kalyanaraman at the bell-ringing ceremony held as part of Kalyan Jewellers' IPO listing at the National Stock Exchange, Mumbai, on 26 March 2021.

T.S. Kalyanaraman with his family.

Finally, he was convinced that he was going to be the campaigner for not just a brand but an institution, as well as a progressive movement.

We did not ask Bachchan sir to say, 'Buy gold from Kalyan Jewellers . . .' Rather, we wanted him to be the main teacher to give the right impetus to the campaign for bringing transparency to the jewellery sector. He understood what we said. 'You are doing a lot of good things. Congratulations! I will join you,' he said.

Amitabh Bachchan, the man, never moved an inch from what he said—he continues to endorse Kalyan Jewellers.

16

The Memory of Waves

Today, Amitabh Bachchan is not just the champion of our advertisements. He is the patriarch of the Kalyan Jewellers family. A professional relationship that turned into family bonding.

He has been to our house in Thrissur many times in the past eight years. In the beginning, he was our guest. It's a rarity. Bachchan sir's presence in a very personal place, such as coming over to our home, did not happen suddenly.

Today, Bachchan sir comes home not as a guest but as the patriarch of a family. When he comes home, it is as though the head of the family has arrived. Bachchan is a stickler for punctuality. A day for him begins in the puja room, after which he comes to the dining hall as one among us and has his breakfast. The person who comes for inaugurations is far removed from the person who comes home. At home, he is one of us.

Bachchan sir is very disciplined and has his own routine. When it comes to food, once he's had his quota, no amount of persuasion will sway him—even if it was the tastiest dish in the world. He swears by his menu. No temptation can ever conquer his determination. Once he's decided, there is no turning back.

Despite his age, there is no personality as dedicated as him to his profession. We are witnesses to this. Once, he came home during Navratri. It was 10 p.m. when the programme concluded. Bachchan sir was resting in his room. My children and I were beside him. He goes to sleep very late. So, we sat and spoke late into the night.

That day, too, we sat and spoke about family matters and current affairs. It was nearing midnight. 'I shall show you some rushes of my latest movie . . . we will all watch them together . . . call everyone in the house . . .' Bachchan sir said.

Haven't you seen the excitement and joy on children's faces when they score good marks or win prizes in competitions? It was precisely the same excitement and joy that was writ large on Bachchan sir's face.

Bachchan sir was the first to enter the home theatre. He waited patiently for all to come. The special screening began after everyone had entered the room. He asked us to increase the volume. After each scene, he asked us to pause the screening. He would then give a short description of the scene. He would ramble on about the incidents, including jokes, and challenges that occurred during the shooting of the movie. He would narrate even the minutest details. Sometimes, he would ask us to rewind so that he could recollect anything he had left out.

All this while, there would be a strange glow on his face, akin to a child showing the marks on his progress card to his parents. 'Sir, how many times have you seen this?' Ramesh asked.

'I don't know,' he said.

For he had lost count of the times he had seen it. What he said next is something the new generation involved in making movies ought to keep in mind.

'Each time I view it, I get something new which helps me improve my performance the next time.'

These are the words of an actor par excellence who has essayed countless characters and moments on the silver screen for years together, one whose name is synonymous with Indian cinema. It shows the passion and enthusiasm of a person who has seen life for seven decades in his career. Even to this day. 'I'm still learning to act,' he says.

It is this passion that sustains Amitabh Bachchan as Amitabh Bachchan. It's the reason the 'B' in his name stands tall among the others. It's the same passion he has towards Kalyan Jewellers the brand. It is very unlike Bachchan sir to act in an advertisement and leave. Even to this day, he inquires about the response to the advertisement. Was the impact positive or negative? If positive, he wants to know the increase in sales. If negative, he studies the reasons behind it.

During the days of the lockdown, I came to know that Bachchan sir was down with Covid. Immediately, I called up Shweta, his daughter. 'There's nothing to worry about. There are only slight symptoms,' she said. 'He was admitted to the hospital only for better care and treatment,' Shweta said. From that moment, my family and I prayed hard for his speedy recovery. The next day, we learnt that Abhishek Bachchan too was down with Covid. We called up Aishwarya and spoke to her. She sounded very brave. Later, Aishwarya and Aaradhya too contracted Covid. Till the day the Bachchan family left the hospital, Rajesh, Ramesh and I used to inquire about their health daily. It was as if our close relatives had fallen sick. Every single day, we prayed fervently to Lord Rama for their speedy recovery and regaining of health. We knew very well that Lord Rama's blessings would be upon Bachchan sir and his family. For he has a heart of gold.

Bachchan sir had come to the festival at the Sri Ramaswamy temple at Punkunnam in 2016. That was his first private visit to Kerala. When he came home after visiting the temple, I asked him out of curiosity: 'What did you pray for, sir?'

'That there be peace and harmony everywhere . . .' he said.

This is Amitabh Bachchan. A person who loves Kerala, a person who prays '*loka samastha sukhino bhavanthu*', a person who, despite reaching the pinnacle of fame and glory, has his feet firmly on terra firma. Amitabh Bachchan is a simple-hearted man. His presence has truly blessed Kalyan Jewellers. Bachchan sir is a great source of energy.

We too now bask in the power of that energy. We fold our hands before that energy source nonpareil which, while shining bright, radiates that light on to others so that they too may shine. 'Thanks' would be too small a word. We bow down before you.

Yet another person from the Bachchan clan became part of our family—Aishwarya Rai. We approached Aishwarya close on the heels of trying to get Bachchan sir to endorse our brand. We readied a presentation like what we made for Bachchan sir with a slight modification. After having narrated what we told Bachchan sir, we said: 'We believe that the world's most beautiful woman must adorn our jewellery. We can think of no one else but you.'

Aishwarya, after looking at the presentation, did not meet us in person like Bachchan sir. Instead, we had a detailed discussion over the phone and, in fact, she signed the contract before Bachchan sir.

Aishwarya endorsed the brand for three years. She excused herself from our advertisements with an apology when her movie career became more demanding. Yet, in our heart of hearts, Aishwarya is still with us. She sends her greetings on all the auspicious occasions in our family. In return, we keep up our family ties.

We consider it Kalyan Jewellers' stroke of luck and divine intervention to have been able to associate with such geniuses. Neither money nor your charms will make people stand by you. There has to be an element of luck. For that, we bow our heads before the omnipotent God.

17

When Fear Moved Us Forward

We cannot predict the depths of certain relationships. Our ties with Amitabh Bachchan are like this. If you ask me how they became so strong, I don't have an answer. Perhaps the reason could be a meeting of minds.

Let me tell you about a few others with whom we have a special bond. The first name that crosses my mind is Shah Rukh Khan. Certain contingencies bring a sea change to our lives. Mostly without our knowledge.

It happened in 2017. We decided to open three showrooms in Oman. The date: 29 December. We advertised the event in a big way. Amitabh Bachchan would inaugurate the showrooms along with our regional brand ambassadors Prabhu, Nagarjuna, Shivraj Kumar and Manju Warrier. Our advertisements stirred Oman.

The schedule was rolled out. Mabella—3.30, Ruwi High Street—4.30, Oman Avenues Mall Bousher—5.30 . . . Oman was getting ready to witness a never-before-seen confluence of stars. Hence, the media too gave it extensive coverage. Naturally, a huge crowd turnout was expected. It created great excitement as our showrooms were to be inaugurated in the presence of the superstars of Indian cinema.

On the eve of the function, i.e. 28 December, we received a phone call from Bachchan sir's office in the morning. 'He isn't feeling well. His health condition does not permit him to come to the function.' Knowing him, we knew that this decision would have been made by him only.

Great challenges lay ahead. All of Oman was waiting for Amitabh Bachchan. We were unsure how the people would react if they knew he wasn't coming. The more we thought about it, the more it gave us shivers. I had a near-blackout. But I knew the blessings of Lord Sri Rama and our forefathers would come to our aid to overcome any challenge. How true it was!

We put our heads together. If Amitabh Bachchan is not coming, who else would fit the bill? Bachchan sir is irreplaceable. Who else could fill that void even a wee bit? That was our dilemma. 'Shah Rukh Khan!' The idea came from Ramesh. By bringing Shah Rukh Khan, we could, to a certain extent, make up for Bachchan's absence. The idea was acceptable to all. But how?

We knew Shah Rukh Khan. He knew us too. But we were not close enough to invite him to our programme at short notice. Yet, we attempted.

Somehow, I felt this would work out. I've no answer if you ask me why I felt so. On certain occasions, the mind prepares the ground for a bunch of surprises. It was so wild a thought.

'There is no change in the programme,' I told everyone. 'Everything will go as planned.' I asked Ramesh to invite Shah Rukh Khan. Ramesh was doubtful whether the plan would work out. Let us try, I said. If SRK, as the world calls him, said 'Yes,' it would be something great. If he said 'No,' then we shall think of something else. This is what I thought.

Ramesh dialled Shah Rukh Khan's number in Mumbai. Soon, SRK came on the line. He spoke to Shah Rukh Khan in an apologetic tone. For there was great impropriety in calling up such a great actor at the eleventh hour and inviting him to our programme. He explained our predicament and requested SRK to help us out.

Shah Rukh Khan gave him a patient hearing. There was no sign of 'why are you calling me at this eleventh hour' in his voice. Instead, he said calmly: 'Give me some time . . . I shall let you know.' With that, our hopes resurfaced. I knew everything would work out fine, just as I thought.

Shah Rukh's call came at 4 p.m. He was ready! Immediately, I called my secretary and said, 'Send a chartered plane for Shah Rukh Khan. Make all arrangements for him at once. Never compromise on anything . . .'

'Sure, sir. I will soon make the arrangements,' my secretary said. 'But there's an issue, sir. I'm doubtful about the visa. We have hardly an hour. The visa processing office will close at 5 p.m. We have very little time to get the passports of Shah Rukh Khan and his entourage and apply for the visas.'

I did not lose hope. Though my mind faltered in the beginning, I was confident of success in the end. Officials in the visa processing office were ready to wait for us. It is in times like these that we feel God's presence. Or else, how could things that seemed impossible become possible? All our efforts would have gone down the drain if any one officer had said a firm 'no'.

The next day, Shah Rukh Khan appeared before the crowds who were waiting anxiously to see Amitabh Bachchan! The people readily embraced the surprise Kalyan Jewellers had in store for them. There was not a word or murmur. The programmes concluded as gracefully as they had begun.

'I consider Kalyan Jewellers' invitation a big blessing. I am extremely happy to see you all in Muscat. Amitji was supposed to be here today. Unfortunately, he is indisposed. I am as grief-stricken as you all. I now stand in his place. I will convey your regards to him,' Shah Rukh Khan said at his inaugural address.

I had said in the beginning that some relationships are difficult to define. Think of the drama that went into our bonds with Shah Rukh Khan! If you were to show it on the silver screen, would you believe all this happened in real life? Sometimes, certain realities are greater than imagination.

We would have cut a very sorry figure before the people had we sat helpless when Bachchan sir fell ill and could not attend our programmes. It is only because we overcame that fear that we could bring Shah Rukh Khan in place of Bachchan sir. Maybe it was as a reward for our efforts that we could bring Shah Rukh and thus develop a friendship with him.

Fear not, my mind said. I heeded that voice. I realized that along with fear comes the weapons to fight it.

18

We Are a Family

We have brand ambassadors in Hindi, Tamil, Telugu and Kannada languages. In the earlier chapters, I've told you about the paths that led to Bachchan sir. Now, I shall tell you how the others too became a part of the Kalyan Jewellers family.

The people of Tamil Nadu are particular about their language, and it is part of their cultural identity. Though the people passionately embrace modernism in all its aspects, they closely guard their relationship with the Tamil tradition and see family as the foundation for success in their lives.

As we opened newer showrooms in Tamil Nadu, the need for a brand ambassador became imperative. We needed to do in Tamil Nadu the same things we did in Kerala with the help of movie stars. We began a hunt for a movie star. Our search yielded results. We got a name: Prabhu.

Prabhu had wide acceptance among the people of Tamil Nadu as the son of Sivaji Ganesan. Sivaji Ganesan was a cult figure in Tamil Nadu. The sheen of the silver screen and his life had created a halo of sorts around him. Sivaji Ganesan has a revered place in the hearts of the people of Tamil Nadu. Prabhu carried the torch of that shining legacy.

We got in touch with his brother Ramkumar, who was managing Prabhu's affairs. Ramkumar's response dimmed our hopes. Not a single movie star has appeared in any jewellery advertisements in Tamil Nadu, Ramkumar said. MGR, Sivaji Ganesan, Rajinikanth, Kamal Haasan, considered role models of the people, haven't acted in advertisements. Hence, Ramkumar was sceptical of a personality like Prabhu taking such an adventurous step. Ramkumar was doubtful whether Prabhu's fans would approve of their role model acting in advertisements. To those who love Prabhu, he is not a mere movie star. He is the great son bearing the legacy of illustrious actor Sivaji Ganesan. Prabhu fans gave immense value to that legacy. Despite being weighed down by such thoughts, Ramkumar arranged a meeting with Prabhu.

Prabhu was reticent by nature. It wasn't easy for him to strike up a conversation. Prabhu spoke of the advertisements of various jewellers in Tamil Nadu. Most of them were jingles. Towards the end of such advertisements, TV stars or models used to name the jewellery shop and request that people buy jewellery from them. Prabhu said he wasn't interested in such advertisements. He made it clear such advertisements did not suit his image. We explained to him at length our advertisements featuring Mammootty and somehow convinced him. We also spoke to him about how, over the years, we could win the confidence of the people in the jewellery business. He agreed when we told him he needed to be just himself and not one making a bid to sell Kalyan's jewellery.

We followed it up with more meetings and cleared his doubts. Finally, he agreed to be our brand ambassador. We hoped for a contract of three years. Seeing his reticent nature and style, we requested him to be our ambassador for at least a year. He nodded. The advertisement featuring Prabhu became an instant hit in Tamil Nadu. And so, the people there too began to repeat our slogan, 'Trust—is everything.'

Our ties with Prabhu were akin to finding a treasure. We consider it a boon from the Almighty. Prabhu appeared in many Kalyan Jewellers' advertisements and inaugurated around seventy showrooms. No brand ambassador in the world has, arguably, opened so many showrooms—a world record of sorts.

Whenever we are in Chennai, we go to his house, have lunch and exchange pleasantries with him. And it's vice versa. Prabhu comes to our house whenever he is in Kerala. He is a part of our family now. Seeing our closeness, many in Tamil Nadu felt that Prabhu owned Kalyan Jewellers!

Prabhu's love and affection towards Kalyan Jewellers are clear in his words. To a question about his relationship with Kalyan, Prabhu said: 'I'm a brand ambassador of Kalyan Jewellers. The reason for Kalyan Jewellers' growth in ten to fourteen years is the love, affection and trust of the people. For this, I must thank the people. Many people say Kalyan Jewellers belongs to me, but it is not mine. I'm a brand ambassador. Kalyan family is like my family.'

It was pretty much in the same way that Telugu actor Nagarjuna and Kannada actor Shivraj Kumar joined our team. The discovery of Prabhu made us scout for stars in the other two south Indian languages. This was in 2008. We had scheduled the inauguration of our showrooms in Bengaluru and Hyderabad for two consecutive months. In both places, we were on the lookout for suitable personalities who could be presented before the people. Here, too, we opted for the same yardstick we used in Tamil Nadu.

Like the people of Tamil Nadu, those in Andhra Pradesh and Karnataka attach great value to tradition. That's why we wanted someone like Prabhu, who had a rich tradition to speak of. It's precisely for the same reason we considered Rajkumar's son Shivraj Kumar and Nageswara Rao's son Nagarjuna.

However, none of them had acted in an advertisement. Convincing Nagarjuna and Shivraj Kumar was half as difficult as getting the assent of Prabhu. One after another, they signed the contracts. Nagarjuna and Shivraj Kumar, whom we call 'Nag sir' and 'Shivanna', are now part of our family, like Bachchan sir and Prabhu. Our bonds have grown beyond the definition of a company and its brand ambassadors.

Let me now come back to a person from Kerala—Manju Warrier. She became part of the Kalyan family through sheer coincidence. It was the time Manju was returning to the stage through a dance recital after a sabbatical from her acting career. We can say with pride that the second phase of the highly talented actor began with Kalyan Jewellers.

And so, Manju Warrier donned the grease paint once again. This time, along with none other than Amitabh Bachchan at the Mumbai Film City. No other actor in Malayalam had garnered as much media attention for her grand re-entry to the silver screen as Manju Warrier.

It's been eight years since we began our ties with Bachchan sir. Our bonds with Prabhu go as far back as fifteen years. As for Nag sir and Shivanna, it's been twelve years. All of them are our great friends now. I've said this many times over. They are part and parcel of our family. According to Guru Rabindranath Tagore, one needn't be friends for a long time to develop a deep-rooted friendship. How true were his words!

Celebrities are not the only ones who are part and parcel of the Kalyan Jewellers family. For years together, around 100 people have been part of Kalyan Jewellers' 'core team'. They are people who joined our team at some point in time and become an integral part of our family. From managers to drivers, each had the opportunity to leave us but never did. All of them are with us, even to this day.

I'd consider this sheer luck. You cannot buy the trust of the employees merely by giving them a handsome salary. Over and above that, certain things will make them want to stay with you. One of them is luck.

It is these 100 people who lead Kalyan Jewellers forward. They can speak their mind on any matter. We have even given them the freedom to criticize us. Outsiders look on in disbelief at the freedom our employees enjoy. 'How is it possible?' many think.

The employees take this freedom not to get their things done. Rather, it is for the good of the company. The many years of service have made them feel the company belongs to them. So, we must know their needs and do what is needed. For the employees will not speak for themselves.

Giving them freedom doesn't mean they will assume they have the power to do anything or do things according to their whims and fancies. They are ready to do anything for the good of the company. It's not enough that only customers have faith in you. The employees, too, must repose their faith in you. Our employees conduct themselves as my children and I do. It is not something that we have taught them. It is something that they learnt by themselves.

As far as possible, we try to understand our employees and gauge their fortitude and attitude. From this, we make certain discoveries. One among the 100 people who now lead Kalyan Jewellers was once upon a time a worker at my home. I had discovered a spark and a fire in him. That led me to think he was meant for greater heights in life.

I slowly shifted him to our showroom. He did not belie my hopes. He proved his mettle. So, from salesman to senior salesman and from there to branch manager and regional manager, he grew by leaps and bounds. He's now in charge of an entire region.

19

To My Fellow Travellers, with Love

Once, I was travelling by plane to Dubai. I looked through the window. The clouds were drifting backwards as we moved forward. Some were floating around like milkweeds. The plane seemed like a bird caught in a swirl of milkweed. I was lost in thought as I sat in the aircraft's belly. Such sights take us back in time. The faces of several people who had journeyed with me so far appeared before me.

As I pen my thoughts now, I feel I'm airborne among the milkweed clouds again. My mind takes me back to that journey and the faces that appeared before me that day. The same faces appear before me now— faces from the past that tell a story of Kalyan (including me). The role they played in the journey of Kalyan Jewellers, from the past to the present, is not insignificant. My story wouldn't be complete without a few words about them. For they were fellow travellers. Some, even to this day.

It's the story of a journey. Some people had begun the journey with us. Some joined us midway. Some left. Some people who had been with us from the outset are still with us. So there is no point in saying the journey is incomplete. I remember only the journey and the varied experiences. Those who journeyed with us and left us at some point in time form part of the narrative. I feel proud to have journeyed with them for quite some distance. Though they aren't with me now, I fondly recall my association with them. I treasure memories of the days I spent with them.

The growth of any organization depends on the foundation laid by its very first employees. It reaches the pinnacle of growth with their toil and sweat. But, sad to say, many of them leave for various reasons either during the organization's growth or when it has reached its zenith. It wasn't so with Kalyan Jewellers. I'd call it providence or sheer luck. Our very first employees are with us even to this day.

Sunny was the first person to join me at Kalyan Jewellers. He is the first among the over-8000 employees. Sitaraman, Chidambaran and Ravindran are still with us. Sunny was in charge of purchases. No narrative about our early days would be complete without the mention of Sangameshwaran alias 'Sangam'. Sangam, who had been with us for a very long time, is now indisposed and at home. I visit him from time to time. Kalyan Jewellers' family members remember with gratitude the services he has rendered to the company.

More employees joined the fold when we began our showroom in Palakkad. They were Mani, Paulson, Mahadevan, Baiju, Ramesh Kumar, Sojan, Suresh, Ayyappan, Moorthy, Johnson, Sebastian, Jose and Sunil Kumar. All of them joined the organization when we simultaneously opened showrooms in Palakkad and Perinthalmanna. Sunny is not with us now. He retired from Kalyan Jewellers after years of exemplary service. But the footprints of excellence he left behind still exist as an asset to the organization and an inspiration to many.

The rest are still members of the Kalyan family. It means they have been with us for a great part of their lives. I'd say they have offered their own lives to Kalyan.

Those who had begun their careers as salesmen now hold top posts in Kalyan. Don't call it promotions. Rather, they are rewards for their dedication and hard work.

Mani is in charge of a part of Kalyan's global gold purchases. Paulson looks after another part. The silver jewellery section is under Sitaraman while Baiju is in charge of the diamond purchases section. The responsibility of looking after the Maharashtra–Gujarat sector lies with Mahadevan. Ramesh Kumar holds charge of the Kerala sector while Jose is in charge of Karnataka. The responsibility of the sourcing division rests with Sunil Kumar. Johnson, Sebastian, Chidambaram and Ravi hold prominent responsibilities at Kalyan's Thrissur headquarters. Sojan left for his heavenly abode while discharging his duties at Kalyan. It was akin to a painful jab during a journey. We feel a certain vacuum when we go back in time to our memories.

Suresh and Ayyappan are secretaries to my children. Ayyappan is with Rajesh while Suresh is with Ramesh. I would say they are an extra pair of hands for my sons. Moorthy helps Ramesh in the office as his private secretary. Ravi, my secretary, too, qualifies for the same description as Suresh and Ayyappan. The years that passed have given each one of our first line of employees a new role to play. From their roles behind the sales counter, all of them have moved on to shoulder crucial responsibilities in the organization. Much water has flowed under the bridge. But one factor remains unchanged. Their unflinching loyalty to Kalyan Jewellers. The passing years have only added to the sparkle.

There is something that happens in every family business. There will be a handful of elderly employees who are dear to the older generation. When the baton of business changes hands from the old generation to the new—from grandfathers and fathers to the children—the elderly employees are slowly eased out of the business. Fresh faces, mostly candidates of the children, occupy their place.

It wasn't so in our case. We began our innings together. Those with us now have been with Ramesh, Rajesh and me right from the beginning. There was no generation gap. We began as a team and continue as a team.

Time has changed Kalyan's style of functioning. A chain of professionals has joined our ranks. They are the roof of our structure—our shield while facing the toughest challenges. Standing as pillars of support to the roof and the structure are our first line of employees. The strength they give us is beyond compare. It is their fortitude that keeps Kalyan Jewellers going.

I would call it luck. Or maybe providence. For it's tough to get a trustworthy workforce like this. They could have left Kalyan Jewellers for greener pastures. Several opportunities had come their way. But they decided to remain with the company.

From the outset, I used to give handsome salaries and unbridled freedom to the employees. My initial plan was to open just three or four showrooms and stop with that. But, within a short period, Kalyan Jewellers came to occupy the pride of place among the prominent names. Naturally, the recognition of Kalyan raised the 'market value' of its employees. As the company expands, so will the reputation and value of its workforce. 'There are innumerable opportunities outside the company for all of you to grow. I will not be a hindrance to your dreams. It's easy to get a job in any of the reputed companies. Those who want, can leave and join elsewhere where they feel their future is more secure,' I had told my employees when I had just three or four showrooms in mind. But everyone said in unison: 'No, we are not leaving. We would stay with you.'

It is precisely this mindset that I referred to as luck or providence. The decision of the employees did not lead them to bad times. Instead, it kept them in good stead all these years. Rather, a part of the company's reputation clings on to the workforce—something they can say with pride. It probably could be the remuneration for oodles of self-confidence.

I consider all those who work with us as our children. I'm not boasting. Ask anyone who works with Kalyan Jewellers. My children and I take part in all the staff meetings. My children speak only of their business and the targets to be achieved. There's no point in blaming them for that. It's the need of the hour in an age of fast-paced competition. One can survive only by thinking along the same lines. It's because my children concentrate on our business that I can deal with my employees on another level. What's most important is safeguarding personal relationships. At our meetings, I speak up only after everyone else has had their chance to speak. I don't allow anyone to change the agenda of the meeting or grant special favours because I am present at the meeting.

'Forget what Rajesh and Ramesh said.' This is the first thing I say when my turn comes to speak. 'You must first look after your family. You are working for them. There is no point in working without giving a thought to your family. You must take time off your work and spend quality time with your family. After family, comes health. Never neglect your health for work,' is what I tell them. 'How many leaves have you taken?' I ask some employees. To please me, they say: 'We've not taken any leave, sir . . .' 'That's not right,' I tell them at once. 'How can you forget your family and work here? Who compelled you to do so?'

There would be a big round of applause after I had spoken. Often, many would say even their fathers wouldn't have spoken affectionately to them.

I don't make any of my colleagues who wish to see me wait. Anyone can come and meet me directly without taking an appointment. If anyone comes to see me bypassing the hierarchy, then it has to be something really important. Maybe he has a question only I can answer. It may be family issues, monetary matters or some vexed official matters . . . If not for him, for whom should I keep the doors of my office wide open?

Not just our employees but anyone who has cooperated with Kalyan Jewellers at least once will treasure the relationship. So is the case with those who associate with us in business, especially our suppliers. Among them are four or five names who have been with us from the time we set out on the 'golden route'. We remember with gratitude those who offered us credit when we were just a small shop. Though we had returned the money within the stipulated time, our obligation towards them is like an outstanding debt.

The distributors of yesteryear still supply jewellery to us. One among them is Sundaram of Coimbatore. Today, his grandchildren give us the material. The business may have changed hands, from grandfather to grandchildren. But the ties are still strong. KVR, who makes bangles, Praveen from Mumbai and Om Prakash are the others on the list. All of them had helped us in the past. Today, we can be of help to them. We could have gone in search of many distributors. We never did that. It is solely because of our obligation to them. Like an outstanding debt.

Sivadasan and V.A. Sreekumar come to my mind when I think of my associates who are not with me now. Sivadasan was the interior decorator of our first line of showrooms. He bid goodbye to Kalyan Jewellers and entered the furniture business. Sreekumar made ad films for us in our initial days. When moviedom beckoned him, he moved on to pursue that.

Those who joined hands with us continue to do so. What gives our feet strength is the fact that their numbers far outweigh those who left us. There are many more miles to go, says an inner voice. I pray that we have the mental and physical strength to carry on. Any journey becomes a pleasure when you have with you people whom you can trust. I have a wealth of people whom I can bank on. So, fearlessly, I continue my onward journey.

20

My Neighbourhood Friends

Kalyan Jewellers introduced many things to its customers. Though revolutionary experiments, they were all close to our hearts. If you ask me what's most unique about them, my opinion would be My Kalyan centres. It could, arguably, be the first such concept in the global jewellery business scene.

The concept was born out of a question: How can we offer a more intimate experience to our customers, and become their jeweller of choice? We put our thinking caps on. The answer was 'My Kalyan'. The year was 2010. In those days, very few people came to Kalyan Jewellers from the villages. All of them did their shopping at the small jewellery shops in their neighbourhood. Most of these shops were selling inferior quality gold and customers were unaware of this practice.

As the villagers were sceptical of travelling to the cities for their shopping needs, they relied on whatever was available at hand—even for weddings.

We did educational campaigns about pricing and gold quality in the newspapers and on TV. But we knew that people still had their doubts and no means to clear them. That's how the concept of My Kalyan evolved. It started as a neighbourhood store or you can call them our marketing offices. The idea was that the villagers could reach out to us and have a conversation, clear their doubts and learn more about the purity of gold and BIS hallmarking. This was our novel concept.

The majority of jewellery shopping relates to celebrations such as weddings, and our aim was to reach out to these potential buyers and educate them about the malpractices in the gold industry.

Our modus operandi was very simple. We established contact with wedding venues, beauty parlours and astrologers. For they are the first people who come to know of weddings in the area. Armed with the information, My Kalyan centre staff visited various houses and introduced Kalyan Jewellers to them. Along with inviting the villagers to our shop, the staff members briefed them about the malpractices in the trade.

The villagers who shied away from our 'big shop' could not believe their eyes when they found a My Kalyan staffer at their doorstep. With that, their fear was gone. Soon, we became their trusted neighbour—just as we had envisaged.

We opened 101 My Kalyan centres in Kerala on a single day. There are around 2000 employees in our My Kalyan centres alone. They interact with around one crore people a year. It may sound unreal but that's the truth. When I say 30 per cent of our total revenue comes from My Kalyan centres, imagine how integral the centres are in our business framework!

My Kalyan centres turned beneficial when we opened showrooms outside Kerala. Especially in Tamil Nadu, Andhra Pradesh and regions north of the Vindhyas. The villages in these parts of the country have no access to what's happening in the cities. If you open a showroom in Erode, chances are no news of it will reach the villages. I'm glad we could reach out to the far-flung areas through My Kalyan centres and introduce ourselves to the people there.

The concept of My Kalyan centres was a unique business strategy not only in the jewellery sector but also in the national business scenario. Normally, consumers go in search of traders. Here, traders take their trade right to the doorsteps of the consumers.

Let me conclude this chapter with a narrative of an advertisement we did a decade ago to herald the advent of our My Kalyan centres. The story begins on the doorstep of a house. A girl bids goodbye to her mother and goes to school. On the school bus sits a girl holding two lollipops in her hand and guarding the seat next to her with her bag. She forbids the girl, who gets on to the bus from the next stop, from sitting next to her. She's expecting another friend. Soon, she comes and the two friends happily go to school, nibbling at the lollipops in their hands.

Bags in hand, they enter the class together. When the teacher asks questions, both of them raise their hands in unison to answer them. They play together, laugh together and share their joys. When one girl gets down at her stop from the bus, the other waves goodbye.

But, the next day, she doesn't board the bus. Her friend is upset. She feels all alone. That day, she remains silent in class. She hangs her head down while all others raise their hands to answer the teacher's questions. Her friend's seat remains vacant.

In the evening, as she comes home from school with her mother, she sees household goods being unloaded from a vehicle in the next compound. Her face lights up when she sees her friend playing next door. Smiles burst on their faces like the opening of flowers. She runs to meet her friend. The words we hear are . . .

'Happiness is when those whom we consider our own come near us . . .'

21

A Marital Tie

It happened in 2015. For the first time, Kalyan Jewellers had a partner—someone to share our joys and sorrows and profits and losses. This was Warburg Pincus.

No scripting of Kalyan's history or penning of my life history will be complete without an important chapter about our relationship with Warburg Pincus. Their coincidental arrival helped rebuild Kalyan Jewellers' image worldwide.

Warburg Pincus is a private equity company headquartered in New York. Founded by Eric Warburg in 1939, it was known as E.M. Warburg & Co. In the post-War period, the company functioned in a small way with twenty employees. The company came to be known as E.M. Warburg Pincus & Co. after it merged with Lionel I. Pincus & Co. in 1966. Lionel Pincus took over the company's reins after E.M. Warburg demitted office in 1965. The company made its presence felt in the private equity sector with the arrival of John Vogelstein. Warburg Pincus began investments in Europe in 1983 and, in 1994, it opened an office in Asia. Today, Warburg Pincus has investments worth $72 billion in 845 companies in forty countries.

Warburg got in touch with us in 2014. It is not merely our achievement in the jewellery business that led them to us. It's the image Kalyan Jewellers had—a company doing jewellery business honestly and transparently for years together—that brought Warburg Pincus to us. The bigwigs who have for long played in the international arena know very well that doing honest business in gold is no child's play. They will not associate themselves with anyone engaged in shady deals. They will not strike a deal with anyone having a tainted reputation.

Warburg decided to invest in Kalyan Jewellers after studying the company closely for a year. It offered to invest Rs 1200 crore. The growth attained after investing for five to six years can be achieved in a year with a one-time investment, Warburg representatives said. At a glance, we found it to be right. At that time, Kalyan Jewellers needed five to six years to invest Rs 1200 crore. Here was a group telling us it would fund us in one go! Anyone else in our place would have fallen for that offer and pocketed the amount. Not us. We look before we leap.

At such critical junctures, I consult my children. Of course, I have to consider their opinions. In the case of Warburg too, we put our heads together. My children were sceptical of such a move. 'Should we?' they asked. They had a valid reason. Till that moment, we were the sole owners of the title 'Kalyan Jewellers'.

The company was so close to our hearts that we could not imagine someone else coming on board as a partner. No matter how many times we gave it a thought, our answer would be a definite 'no'.

To convince my children, I gave them an example. It was about their sister—my daughter Radhika. 'I know you love your sister dearly and would hate for her to marry and move away from home. Yet, it is your responsibility to get her married. Nature has willed the change. You must be prepared to accept that. The same is true of Kalyan as well—by holding tight, we would only be stifling the growth of the brand. The time is right to onboard a partner and if you truly love the brand, you will accept this change. There is nothing to worry about here.'

My children got the message. That didn't mean we would rush through things and welcome them in. We inquired thoroughly about Warburg Pincus. We had to make sure they had the same temperament as ours. In a marriage proposal, it's natural to make inquiries about the boy and his background. Isn't it important to know whether it's a match for us?

Consider this: We are travelling by car. En route, someone gets into the car. We'd like to go at a speed of 80 kmph. That's our style. We've conditioned our vehicle to travel at that speed. We don't like to drive at a greater speed. What if the person who got into your car asks you to drive at 120 kmph? That would destroy our peace of mind and kill the sheer joy of travelling. We will be in deep trouble if the person who gets into our car does not have the same temperament as us.

We should let in only those people who find joy in travelling in our car, at our speed and on the same route. Otherwise, we'd have to listen to them and accept what they say. So, before giving a lift to wayfarer Warburg in our Kalyan car, we made ourselves very clear on certain points. Our destination and our preferred pace of travel. Not a single employee, including our staff, is to be changed. We can move forward only according to our style of functioning.

But you can offer suggestions. In areas where we are ignorant, you can advise and even correct us. If only you can agree to these points, do we need a partner. Call it our luck, Warburg also had a similar outlook.

'Remain with us for some time. Learn about us.' This was what we told Warburg. After a while, neither you nor we should feel we shouldn't have got into this. The relationship shouldn't fall apart after, say, three or four months or one or two years.

Luckily, the ways of Warburg and Kalyan were the same. Slow, mature, never greedy, those who love their brand to the hilt. The perfect partner.

There are two types of growth. In an earlier chapter I had said, if you want to start getting returns from a market like the Middle East, you may have to be patient and wait for a few years before turning a profit.

But few think along the same lines. If they spend Rs 10 today, they want it back tomorrow. Short-term thinking. Not long-term.

This is not our line of thinking. We never thought about a particular day. We thought ahead—beyond ten years, perhaps. It's difficult to do business with someone who invests money today and seeks profit the next day. We have a vision. If the other person thinks contrary to our plans, then we cannot accept money from them. We were very frank in our statements. We explained to Warburg our projects and asked them if they were acceptable to them. 'We think alike,' Warburg said. 'We too share the same vision. Let's move forward in a transparent and trustworthy manner. There is no need for haste. We shall sit in the rear. You may drive your vehicle at your comfortable speed,' Warburg said.

That's how Warburg joined hands with us. It's been six years now. There has never been a discordant note. There is a cinematic term— 'director's actor'. It means an actor who acts exactly as the director wants. In much the same way is Warburg—a 'promoter's investor'. We consider it our luck to have got such a fine, suitable investor.

I had said earlier that the initial investment was Rs 1200 crore. As our credibility rose, Warburg invested an additional Rs 500 crore in Kalyan Jewellers after three years.

22

Objects of Necessity, Not Luxury

When we speak of desires, we always refer to the sky as the limit. To be very honest, let me tell you, we never wanted to grow and touch the sky. A company that functions well, a better life, efficient children—that's all I had in mind. But when I dreamt small, God gave in abundance and made us grow as far as the sky! It's all His blessings.

The people of Kerala stared in disbelief when Kalyan Jewellers bought an aircraft in 2012. 'Kalyan—an office that flies' was what the media said. We didn't buy the aircraft to show off our pomp and grandeur. Rather, we bought it when at one stage it became a necessity.

Let me recount an incident that happened a couple of years ago. Kalyan Jewellers was planning to buy an aircraft. A lot of calculations had to be done. Anxiety was writ large on our faces. For we were preparing to touch the sky. On one of those stressful days, as I lay down to sleep at night, the face of a small boy appeared before me. My friend, who had studied with me in Class VII. Along with his memory, came that day . . .

I was in a jovial mood that day. I had a precious gift in my bag when I went to school—a battery-operated aeroplane made of plastic which my father had bought from Mumbai. I would feel my bag from time to time to see if it was still there . . .

I waited for lunchtime and I took the aeroplane out of my bag, in much the same way a magician pulls out a hare from his hat. Those who were in a mad rush to have their lunch crowded around me. They forgot their hunger when they saw the magical object in my hands.

Some felt it. Others smelled it. The entire class stared in wonder as the plane began moving on the floor. In no time, the classroom turned into one big aerodrome. The students clapped their hands and jumped up excitedly as if to welcome the first motorized bird to the class.

As the bell went, the plane returned to my bag as magically as it had appeared. I returned from school like a victorious hero. It was then I noticed him at the entrance to the school. He was waiting for me. I had seen him among those who screamed ecstatically in the classroom during lunch break. He was one of my dear friends. He held my hand, looked me in the eye and asked: 'Will you give me that aeroplane?' I clasped my schoolbag tightly and held it close to my body. I could feel his grip tightening on my bag.

'I shall show it to everybody at home and bring it back,' he said. 'Give it to me for a day,' he said. He was on the verge of tears. His mood had changed from longing for an object to sheer desperation. I felt sad. Tears welled up in my eyes. I took the plane out of my bag. My friend's face lit up as if a thousand crackers had burst in front of him. Before I could open my mouth to say anything, he snatched the plane from my hands and ran away.

I couldn't sleep that night. I waited with bated breath for dawn to break. I never spoke a word of it to anyone at home lest I get a dressing down. 'Where's my plane . . .' I asked my friend as soon as I saw him the next day. The previous day's expression had gone from his face. In its place was an expression of nonchalance. 'I forgot,' he said without batting an eyelid. Saying this, he ran away and was soon lost among his friends.

In the days that I followed, I repeated my question and he, his answer. A week later, I broke the news to my father. I thought he would fly into a rage. Instead, he stroked my back and said, 'Never mind. Let him take it . . . we will buy a new one.'

As days passed, I forgot about the incident. We played in the school compound as usual. It was after so many years that I boarded the toy plane and went back to my childhood. That night, I slept with a smile on my lips.

We decided to buy a plane when we had twenty-three showrooms in both Kerala and Tamil Nadu. It was the time we were thinking of branching out to Karnataka and Andhra Pradesh—a time when we were slowly nurturing Team Kalyan as a brand. Mobility was of paramount importance. Our showrooms were spread all over south India, and we had to reach each place fast. There's no point in opening showrooms if you can't manage them accurately and efficiently.

You need about Rs 30–40 crore to set up a showroom. Our idea was to set apart the amount needed to start a showroom to buy an aircraft. The plan was to minus one showroom from the total number of showrooms we were planning to open. We could concentrate more on south India.

An aircraft for Kalyan Jewellers was Ramesh's idea. He argued that in the coming years, Kalyan would expand by setting up more showrooms and, without speedy access to these places, managing things would become very difficult. With an aircraft, we could attain great heights, he said.

The idea of having our aircraft took my mind back by thirty-seven years. Like the other businessmen, I too wanted to fly on a plane. And, when I flew for the first time to Mumbai in 1982 on a Rs 480 ticket, it was as if I had conquered the sky. 'With this, our business must improve,' was all my father said while giving me the money for the ticket.

Now, here I was, someone who wanted to board a plane just once in life, looking at buying an aircraft during his sunset years. Call it a twist of fate. What else can one say! I told my sons what my father had told me then: 'Buy it only if it will further our business. It should not be to squander away our money.'

'Think not about how much it would cost to buy an aircraft. Nor think about the expenses we would incur for travelling by plane. Rather, think about the profit we can make by using the aircraft. Think about how many hours or days we can save if we travel by air. Think about the places that can be accessed and how it will help our business, how it will benefit us in the future . . .' These are the things that you must keep in mind, I told my sons.

Rajesh didn't agree to the proposal. But I was on the same page as Ramesh. My words made Rajesh think. He made his calculations. Later, he changed his mind. Rajesh found we could save many days of travel, which would ultimately benefit our business.

Take, for example, our showrooms in Kadapa or Kurnool. Eight years ago, there wasn't any connectivity as we have now. It would take two days to reach there. Once there, there would be work only for two or three hours. It was for this we were spending two days on travel. Or take the case of Hubli in Karnataka. There's a flight to Hubli at 9 a.m. The next flight is at 6 p.m. Both flights operate only for two days a week. So, the only way out was to travel by car from Bengaluru. Now, that would consume nine whole hours! Strangely, there is not a single flight to Belgaum. It would take days to reach there. All this hardship for a few hours of work!

That's why we decided to buy an aircraft. We were ready to overlook the expenses if our income would rise. We bought a four-seater Phenom 100 jet from Brazil and made full use of it. Our travels increased, as the plane helped us to get to our destinations with ease.

But it would land only at airports. We'd drive down to Kochi airport from our house in Thrissur and take off from there in our aircraft. Those days, we used to travel at least twice a week by air. It would take two hours from our house to get to the airport and vice versa. That would add up to eight hours a week—which is the time we normally spend in our office on any day. By a rough calculation, almost a day is lost in travelling.

Reaching Hubli and Mysore was not an issue as they had small airports. But, as we expanded to the interior villages of Andhra Pradesh, our travel became arduous. For there were no small airports there. Either we had to abandon expanding into the interior villages or we had to be prepared for the long haul.

When travel by road to and from Kochi airport and to our showrooms in the interior villages of Andhra Pradesh became a challenge, we decided to buy a helicopter. We bought the chopper within two years of buying the aircraft. In these two years, the number of our showrooms had jumped from twenty-three to fifty. What made this possible was our effortless journey from one place to another by plane. This made us think. Wouldn't we be able to expand our business further if we bought a helicopter to gain access to remote areas? The seven-seater (including the pilots) Bell 429 copter took us swiftly to places inaccessible by plane. It cut short our travelling time.

A year after buying the chopper, the skies beckoned us again. It was the time the Warburg investments were coming in. That was the time we began expansion to the Middle East and Gujarat. The journey of one to one and a half hours stretched to five or six hours. When we had just twenty-three showrooms, it was enough if only the three of us travelled. As the number of showrooms increased, the need to take senior members of the staff looking after a particular state or area to the various showrooms arose too. That was when we thought about a bigger aircraft.

A year after buying the helicopter, we booked a bigger aircraft— the Emperor Legacy 650 IS jet. It cost us Rs 230 crore. The plane made headlines as it touched down at Nedumbassery. We had to convert the forty-seater plane into a thirteen-seater to set up an office and various other rooms.

Today, Kalyan Jewellers has three aircraft. These were all purchased for specific purposes. Call it circumstantial pressure. We travel by bigger aircraft to places where there are large airports and we use the smaller aircraft to reach places where there are only small airports. The helicopter takes us to places where there are no airports at all.

The decision to buy the aircraft played an important role in Kalyan's developmental path and my personal life. Today, we reap its benefits. From the young man who boarded his first flight on a Rs 480-ticket to one who owns three aircraft—I've come a long way. No, it has not made me arrogant. Rather, I bow my head in reverence before that power that has made it all possible. Nothing was predetermined. Everything happened by chance. Even the decisions were taken by someone else. I am but a mere instrument in the hands of the One who controls the entire universe. Or I'm at best a puppet. I just let things be. I have no role in anything. It's all fate.

The toy plane of Class VII comes flying to my mind. Today, nothing excites my mind more than that toy plane, which I consider larger than the aircraft that I own now.

23

Forest and Greenery

'What's the secret of Kalyan's success?' It's a question I hear most often in recent times. 'There's no secret,' I would answer. As we say in our advertisement, 'Trust—that is everything.' What led Kalyan Jewellers to the pinnacle of success was indeed our professional approach.

In the early days, after winding up the day's work, we (employees, my children and I) used to gather in the evenings and exchange pleasantries. There would be at the most four or five people. It was a daily affair—call it an exercise. To learn from one another.

These conversations at night benefited us immensely. Through these conversations, we could find out the rights and the wrongs and correct ourselves.

As the number of showrooms increased, my children and I turned busier by the day. Work became so hectic that we couldn't find time to hold conversations with our staff as before. We put in place a hierarchy whereby managers would report to the regional head who would apprise the business head of the matters. Above him, we had the CEO—Sanjay Raghuraman.

* * *

I had said in an earlier chapter that our system operates on two levels. While comparing Kalyan Jewellers to a forest, we can say it comprises the green canopy and the tree trunk. In architectural terms, this becomes the roof and the pillars.

Our long-standing staff are our pillars or the trunk. A team of professionals who joined us later form the green canopy.

There is no dividing rule between the two teams. Will a structure ever exist if there is a separation between the pillars and the roof? In case of emergencies, our first line of employees is free to violate the hierarchical order. That's when they contact us directly. You may think this jumping the hierarchical line will create discord among our professional team. No, never. That's our victory. What's the reason, you may ask. Well . . . that's because we have in place a harmonious mechanism. It is precisely from this mechanism that the mellifluous notes of Kalyan flow to create a soothing song.

But, like elsewhere, here too, there were discordant notes. I'm not denying the fact. What would life be without a bit of cacophonous music? But, to prevent it from escalating into full-blown hostilities, we set in place a mechanism called 'secret ballot'.

I had said earlier we used to summon a meeting of our employees. After the meeting, we would give each one a piece of paper. Anyone was free to comment on the company or the job. They could write anything that came to their mind and put it in a box. They could even write about Rajesh, Ramesh or me. There was no need to reveal their names. For only I would open the box and read the letters. Using this mechanism, I could get to the bottom of a vexing issue and prevent it from developing into full-scale hostility. It was a process of self-examination and correction.

Most often, there would not be any 'wrongdoers'. Only rarely would there be accusations. We would take immediate steps to resolve them.

Kalyan, today, is at the forefront of institutions that give a handsome salary in the jewellery business sector. We give the employees great freedom too. Despite these factors, if an employee decides to leave the organization, it is mostly because of friction between the employee and his immediate boss. It is to find out such frictions that we have put in place the secret ballot system. The superior officer may not have any grudge against the employee. Under certain circumstances, he may have spoken an angry word or taken some hasty action. That anger, in no way, ought to make way for hatred. It is when anger becomes hatred that an employee has thoughts of leaving the organization. Treatment becomes easy with an early diagnosis of the 'disease'. Having a word with the superior officer will wipe out his anger. That's the power of the secret ballot.

I have never lost my temper with any of my employees. For the simple reason that I would not like to be seen as a boss who strikes fear in the hearts of his staff. It's very easy to make them scared. Raising your voice is more than enough. But gaining their respect will take a lifetime. There is no such thing as a fearsome boss in modern management concepts. The boss must be a person who gains the respect of one and all.

I take great care to be impartial to all and acknowledge the services of every employee, no matter what his/her designation.

We have a special personality development programme. Apart from this, we have separate training sessions for various sections. We give the salesmen lessons in proper body language, proper grooming, the art of conversation and how to behave in the presence of customers.

Take the case of pulling a cart. A couple of persons standing in the front will be ready to pull it with all their strength. Persons on either side of the cart may only give a slight push to it. But some people will attempt to pull it backwards. It is to prevent such a situation that we put in place this orientation programme.

Such practices sustain the ecosystem called Kalyan. Let me reiterate the fact that Kalyan is indeed a forest—something that came up on its own. In this forest, you may find animals from a lion to an elephant, tiger, deer and hare. Birds too. It's indeed luck or providence that there are no rumblings in the jungle or a situation where some tear others apart.

Haven't you seen in certain storybooks a jungle where there is a brotherhood of animals, where they live in peace and harmony? Kalyan is one such jungle.

24

Heart of a Family Tree

The other day, my wife shared with me an interesting analogy about the joint family system. In the olden days, joint families were the order of the day. Rather, they were ubiquitous. Families with just one or two members were looked upon as odd.

But, what's the situation today? Joint families are nowhere to be seen. In their place, we have small families. Nuclear families, rather. Today, families with more members are viewed as strange.

I reflected on my wife's words. I could not but agree with her. Before the joint-family system split apart, there was a certain bonding. A bonding as solid as a huge rock. A huge family comprising many families.

A word. Many words form a line. Many lines come together to form a song. Each word, each line of a song has a beauty of its own. The coming together of these words and lines gives a song its beauty. So it is with joint families. One person. Many people come together to form a family. Four or five families make up a joint family. Family members, from a six-year-old to a sixty-year-old, all live together in harmony. Like a melodious song. Joint families have always been a harmonious blend of different ragas.

I consider myself lucky to have been born into one such joint family, to grow up and be part of it for a major part of my life. As far as I can remember, my family and my father's brothers' families all stayed together under one roof. As the patriarch, we had our grandfather. A wonderful comparison comes to my mind. Our joint family is like our country, India. The various families that make up our joint family are the different states. Like any other joint family, unity in diversity was the hallmark of our joint family too.

As years went by, my father's brothers built their own houses. But we remained as one joint family. The splitting of a joint family is akin to the fragmentation of the single-celled amoeba. It regrows into another one. From one joint family into many joint families. Not a single family fades away. Rather, it gives birth to another.

We had grown up by the time my father's brothers shifted to their own houses. Later, my siblings and I had families. Just as I grew up in the company of my cousins, Rajesh, Ramesh and Radhika grew up amid their cousins.

The strength of any joint family is the woman who enters the household through marriage. Since I got married first, Ramadevi naturally became the first woman to enter the family from outside. Later, Anantharaman's wife Lalitha, Pattabhiraman's wife Meera, Balaraman's wife Uma, Ramachandran's wife Latha—all joined our family.

* * *

After my mother's death, Rama became the lady of the house. My brothers' wives unilaterally bestowed the title upon Rama.

Never once have they quarrelled. There have been no ego clashes between them, nor any elements of jealousy. If anyone of them had a vexing problem, it was shared among the others and a solution was found.

Till Balaraman got married, my two younger brothers, their wives and their children stayed with us. With his marriage, they went to their own houses. Ramachandran, who was a bachelor, continued staying with us. Though my three brothers had their own houses, we remained as one family. All our houses were within walking distance.

There were thirteen children in the family. To them, each of our houses was like their own. The kitchens, too, were no exception. We were five fathers and five mothers. With a majority of the children being boys, one could very well imagine the amount of noise they produced! How the women struggled to tame the mischievous boys and settle their quarrels! We fathers never knew the stress and strain of these 'home affairs' as we were tied up with our business in our offices.

All our children went to the same school. I wouldn't be exaggerating if I said each class in the school had a child from our family! Need I say much about the character and conduct of the children of those days? If the teacher rebuked or punished any child, all the other children would patiently wait until evening to rush to their houses and give the 'hot news' to the elders. They wouldn't even wait to enter their houses. As soon as they reached the gates, they would scream at the top of their voices for all to hear!

Though each one would thus make the best use of opportunities to belittle one another, the bonds of friendship between them were rock solid. When Rama went to Madras to see her parents, Rajesh, Ramesh and Radhika would be at one of my brothers' homes. They preferred to stay back and play with their cousins than go with Rama. Rama could peacefully leave on her journey, happy in the belief that the children would be safer here than anywhere else.

In our house, all of us had nicknames. Though they had their origins in the house, the word got out and, even to this day, those close to us call us by our nicknames. I am known as 'Remani'. Anantharaman is 'Ratnam' while Pattabhiraman is 'Ramakrishnan', Balaraman 'Balu', and Ramachandran 'Raju'.

No memory of our joint family would be complete without mentioning the names of two people. Though they never settled down in our home, they were links in our family chain. They were my sisters'

husbands, Venugopal and Srinivasan. Venugopal and Meenakshi stay
in Hyderabad. Geethalakshmi's husband Srinivasan, who belonged to
Palakkad, is no more. His death completely shattered me.

Does a tree feel the pain each time a leaf falls? It's something that's
crossed my mind often. Yes, so I feel. So is the case when a member of
the joint family passes away. Haven't we compared the joint family to
a huge tree? Each death in the family causes grievous pain to the entire
family.

Over the years, many of our family members have gone to the
Great Beyond. Grandfather, mother, father, father's sisters, brothers,
my wife's father, mother, sister's husband . . . so many leaves . . . But
the death of one person, whom I have not mentioned so far, left us
all shattered—even to this day. It's the loss of Meera, my brother
T.S. Pattabhiraman's wife. Her untimely departure still tugs at our
heartstrings and brings tears to our eyes.

Meera fell sick even before she had reached life's halfway mark.
The pain spread to our entire joint family. Those painful years revealed
the intensity of our family bonds. Pattabhiraman's children Prakash
and Mahesh were very small when their mother was taken ill. Rama,
Lalitha, Uma and Latha took turns to care for Meera. Prakash and
Mahesh stayed with us all. Since they always had their cousins to play
with, the children never missed their mother.

We weren't ready to leave my brother and his family to fate. Nor
were we prepared to come to terms with Meera's illness. We stood like
a rock behind Pattabhiraman and Meera in their war against fate.

Meera's illness stretched from days to months to years. Throughout,
we held her hands firmly and stayed by her side. Over the years,
Prakash and Mahesh grew up. Meera could remain with them until
they reached an age where they could fend for themselves. Fate's small
mercies for all the good deeds she had done.

One feels lonely and desperate when one feels there is not a single
shoulder to cry on. Meera was a part of our big family. We took great
care to see that neither Meera nor Pattabhiraman and their children

ever felt lonely in those troubled times. Call it the advantage of our joint-family system.

Though we all live in our separate houses, we continue to enjoy the same bonhomie of being together. Our family ties are very intense. For my brothers, their wives, children and grandchildren, it's the same intensity. The passing of years has not diminished it a wee bit—the reason our family tree still stands sturdy and tall. At the centre of any tree, you will find its pith. You may call it love. I leave it to you. Pith or love. Both are correct.

25

An Ornament Called Family

Of all the things you may have in the world, there is nothing greater than mental peace. If you have a lot of money, but no mental peace, then your life is miserable.

It is the family that lays the foundation for peace and tranquillity in life. There is a certain harmony in the very word 'family'. When this harmony is present in the lives of all the members of a family, family life becomes as beautiful as a symphony. It is when a family loses rhythm that discordant notes crop up, resulting in a cacophony.

A family is an ornament that has to be crafted with utmost care. If you falter, you will be left with a piece of useless metal. The ornament must be one which each family member can wear with great pride. It must enhance the beauty of the one who wears it.

In my story, the concept of family has great importance. It's going to be half a century since I became the patriarch of the family. Forty-eight years! I had said in an earlier chapter how Rama entered my life. Swami Nirmalanandagiri Maharaj comes to my mind when I speak about marital life. His book *Samthruptha Dampathya Vijnanam* speaks about the essential mantras for a successful marital life.

In its first chapter, Swami says, according to the Upanishads, the 'da' sound in *dampatya* stands for *da—datta, da—damyata, da—dayadhvam*. Datta means 'to give' (charity) while damyata denotes 'control' and dayadhvam 'compassion.' To the people who approached him, Lord Prajapati says: 'Give,' meaning to engage themselves in acts of charity. Dampatya is the confluence of three words, namely, *daanam* (charity), *damam* (control) and *daya* (compassion). It means our ancestors had a vision of how sacred a marital life ought to be.

Don't we say 'better half' when we refer to marital life? It originated from the Ardhanareeshwara concept. I take pride in saying my wife constitutes my one-half. My wife has an important role in shaping my personality, shedding new light on my thoughts and showing me the right path.

She has been an influence only on T.S. Kalyanaraman, the husband. She has set free T.S. Kalyanaraman, the businessman.

Once you have entered the business field, put your heart and soul into it. Once you have been a businessman, lose yourself in it.

The world of business is forever hectic. You may not find time for many things in life. Meetings consume most of the time. Certain meetings go on for a whole day. You can never predict when they will end.

What if the better half of a busy businessman is a person with a diametrically opposite viewpoint? That is when you lose your mental peace.

My wife thoroughly knew the businessman in me. I doubt whether Kalyan Jewellers would have scripted such a success story had my better half been a different person.

* * *

Rama and I have three children. My two sons assist me in my business at Kalyan Jewellers. They are my two arms.

There are chances of differences of opinion in business houses either between siblings or between the father and children. I can say with pride that there have been no such differences of opinion either between my sons or between my sons and me. The credit is not all ours. Rather, it's the strength of our family tradition. It has been so ever since the time of our great-grandfathers. Each generation saw and learnt from the previous generation and followed in their footsteps. I'd say we had God's blessings in abundance.

I've never insisted on my children entering the family business. They came on their own. Like me. So, I didn't discourage them. They decided what to study and how to go about it. What next after studies? It's a question they found an answer to. I never raised an authoritarian finger and insisted that they 'do this . . . do that.' They grew up just as new branches sprout on trees.

Today, Kalyan Jewellers is a chariot we draw together. To my left and right are Rajesh and Ramesh. We keep pulling it. We've reached somewhere. Just like a tree that grows upwards . . . I don't know how, if you ask me.

My daughter Radhika is not active in business but is a strong presence that is constant.

Her husband, Karthik, is the son of Dr N.V. Ramani, my wife's brother. What next was the question uppermost in our minds when our jewellery business became a great success. Soon, we came up with an answer: the real estate business. Diversification is a must in the industrial sector. But, if one is not very careful, chances are one could easily burn one's fingers. So, it was after great deliberation that we decided to enter the real estate business. I did not have to think twice about handing over the business to someone. Karthik was the best choice.

Today, the entire responsibility of Kalyan Developers rests on Karthik's shoulders. It's something he does efficiently. Like Kalyan Jewellers, Kalyan Developers too is on the path of growth. Karthik has a place in my heart not as my daughter's husband, but as my son.

It's not one's children alone who have a major role in maintaining harmonious relationships in a family. Those who marry them too play an important role in it. I'm lucky to have got daughters-in-law and a son-in-law who share the same nature as my children. So, when someone asks me, I have no qualms about saying I have six children.

Rajesh and his wife Maya have two children: Rishikesh and Manasa. Ramesh and his wife Deepa have two children: Shivani and Vaishnavi. Radhika and Karthik too have two children: Vikram and Aradhya.

When all of us come together, I am in seventh heaven. Though all of us stay in different houses, all my children visit us daily. On Sundays, we gather at one place and dine together, watch the latest movies and sit and chat together.

When I spend time with my family, I recollect the days I spent in the company of my father and mother. Today, my grandchildren play with mobile phones and computers like toys. Anything in the world is at their fingertips now. This was not the situation in the olden days. My generation grew up playing in the mud and dirt. Those were days of unfettered freedom. It didn't matter whether your friends were rich or poor. We dined at their house and shared food from a single plate.

Tired after a game of football, we children used to drink water from the public taps on the roadside. To cool off, we used to plunge into the ponds and swim for as long as we desired. Not a single illness came anywhere near us. Today, is it possible to even think of those golden days? The world has undergone a sea change. The number of villages has dwindled. Cities have grown by leaps and bounds. Since viruses can attack the body from anywhere, everyone is cautious about their lives. Parents tuck children under their wings and scold them for playing in the mud.

My grandchildren stare in wonder when I tell them this was not the case when I was small. Those good old days of my generation are beyond their comprehension!

Do not stack my thoughts along with cries from various quarters that the past years were the best. I don't attest to that point of view. Everything changes as years go by. So does life and one's perspectives. Accept the best of everything. That's my credo.

This is what I do in my life. Even while embracing the past, I try to imbibe all progressive thoughts, ideas and the growth of present-day life. Nostalgic memories cool my senses and bring a season of spring into my life. But do not chain yourself to the past. That is when you become old-fashioned. You must bring the goodness of the past into the vast openness of the present.

In the olden days, we used to do mental calculations at the textile shop. Close on the heels of the calculator came the computer, which made calculations and stock-taking easy and efficient. The small box stored a wealth of information which otherwise would have required several thousand pages!

I began tackling computers towards the end of the 1990s. It proved too difficult for me in the beginning and took me quite a while to master its technical aspects. A whole new world opened up before me at the click of a mouse—fingers which had till then known only pen, paper and the keys of the calculator. It was unbelievable!

Sitting in my office in Thrissur, I watch in awe as boundaries disappear when I hold videoconferences with Kalyan's employees in different parts of the world. I've heard there's a dark side to technological progress, but it is difficult to forget the positive aspects.

I started speaking about my family, but somehow I digressed and came to the present age. That's how memories are. They take us to different worlds, even without our knowledge. Let me now come back to my family.

A family isn't a system where people are shackled around it. Each member of the family has to have his or her own space. Having one's own space doesn't mean breaking free from the family framework. One should find one's space and share it with others while staying firmly rooted in one's family. It's a kind of sharing of one's freedom too.

In my family, each one has space. As a homemaker, Rama finds happiness in her way. It's the same with my children. In business and my family life, I am not an overbearing father because the need never arose. My family members can read my mind. I too can read their minds. And so, I am extremely rich in mental peace.

26

Our Share of Joy

Let me share with you something that happened in recent times at Kalyan Jewellers and in my life. I was the sole proprietor of Kalyan Jewellers when I set up its first shop. A change of scene for a textile shop owner. It was an adventurous leap. And I didn't miss my mark. Call it divine providence. From a sole proprietorship to having my children join the business and from there to a business partnership with Warburg Pincus—Kalyan Jewellers has come a long way. The challenges and victories have not been mine alone. There has been someone else to share things with. It has been a metamorphosis from the singular 'I' into the plural 'we'.

I had never vowed or desired to single-handedly conquer everything. My guide had always been the words of my grandfather: 'Share what you have!' So, the usual apprehensions of business did not affect me. My children entered the scene not too long after opening Kalyan Jewellers. Much to my relief, they shouldered a major portion of the business, leaving me with just one-third of the responsibilities.

Warburg's arrival gave us a sense of fulfilment. We were happy we had an investor from outside who had full faith in us. By turning Kalyan Jewellers into a global brand, Warburg was only lightening our huge responsibility. It's no mean thing for another to repose full faith in us and undertake the journey; be it life or business. I feel the foremost thing an investor must strive to build is that kind of trust. Trust has a greater value than profit.

It is this point of view that led us to decide on entering the share market. Kalyan Jewellers should not be ours alone. Rather, it must belong to the many thousands who trust us. Isn't this what our grandfather meant by saying 'Share what you have'?

Our relationship with our customers should not be like the casual relationship a jeweller has with those coming to buy ornaments from his shop. For years together, this had been our firm belief. Through selling shares, we were giving it a new expression in today's world.

We had been toying with the idea for a long time. It is only when people have full faith in us that they invest their money in our business. To gain that trust is no mean thing. It takes years of hard work. It's every businessman's dream. With God's blessings and the people's backing, Kalyan Jewellers became an institution synonymous with the word 'trust'. Now, people all over the world think of Kalyan whenever they hear the word 'trust'. Today, 'Isn't trust everything?' is not spoken by Kalyan Jewellers. It's what others speak about Kalyan.

The mental strength we get when we know that the world trusts us is not small. It is when we got that mental strength that we decided to enter the share market. It's good to test the waters before taking the plunge. Before setting out on certain things, one must always study the issues thoroughly.

Several agencies conducted various kinds of studies for us. The preparation and homework went on for two years. Since many are not familiar with the technical aspects of the share market, let me say a few things. I learnt this during the initial public offering (IPO) of Kalyan Jewellers. I'm sharing with you what I learnt during that period. Those who are well-versed in the subject, please excuse me. Though it may offer nothing new to you, I hope it will benefit some. That's all.

When companies want to raise excess capital, they sell their shares in the open market. This is called the initial public offering, or IPO. It's called this as the shares reach the market for the first time. Companies willing to go in for an IPO first select an investment banker. The investment banker assesses the company's assets and puts the records of the company in order before it goes for a public offering. After reaching a consensus on the matter, a draft (draft red herring prospectus also known as DRHP) of the same is presented before the Securities and Exchange Board of India (SEBI), the regulatory body for the securities and commodity market in India. The company, besides stating its current financial position, has to state the purpose for which it is raising additional capital.

Presenting the DRHP is akin to completing the formalities of a wedding. After submitting the DRHP, the company has to wait for two to three months. During this period, SEBI will examine the documents submitted by the company. After getting SEBI's nod, the company has to submit the red herring prospectus (RHP). Once SEBI clears the RHP, the company can enter the share market.

A final decision on entering the share market was taken in February 2020. The DRHP was to be submitted in April. Unfortunately, the coronavirus attack and the subsequent lockdown in March scuttled our plans. For the next three to four months, we had no other option but to sit in our homes like the rest of the world. Should we submit the DRHP after the lockdown is lifted? I discussed the matter with my children, the Warburg officials and other experts. As in any other case, there were two sets of opinions. Our performance would be zero when all our showrooms were closed. Even after lifting the lockdown, we had no clue how the public would respond to our entering the share market for the simple reason we were doing retail business. So, isn't it better to wait for a year? That was what many people told us.

We decided to go ahead and file the DRHP for various reasons. First, after filing the DRHP, as I mentioned earlier, we would get a waiting period of two to three months. Second, we need to go for the IPO only within a year of submitting the DRHP. What if the situations changed during this period? This was what we thought. So, on 24 August 2020, we filed the DRHP.

Here, too, God worked wonders for us. In August, the markets sprang back to life. Our sales graph rose as the jewellery business boomed. Companies enter the share market with IPOs to expand their business. And there is no better time to do so than when business is booming. We had nothing to fear as long as people reposed their faith in us. The time was now ripe.

We got SEBI's clearance in one and a half months, on 15 October 2020. Now, we wanted investors. To find them was a Herculean task. To garner their trust was an even more arduous mission. This is called the roadshow. As part of the roadshow, we had to travel around the globe. We had to fly to the US, the UK, Singapore, the UAE and Hong Kong in search of investors. For that, we had to reveal the company's past, present and future like an autobiography to them. There were a lot of challenges. For jewellers normally don't go in for an IPO. The last time a jeweller went in for an IPO was twenty years earlier!

During the period of Covid, there were restrictions on flights. Hence, a face-to-face meeting with probable investors seemed impossible. How could we get things going without meeting people in person? Help came in the way of technological advancement. Though it helped bring together people who had drifted away because of the Covid scourge, doubts remained. Sitting in front of a computer in my house in Thrissur, we were required to share our details, including history, with people sitting in front of computers elsewhere in the world. How effective would that be, my old-fashioned thinking came to the fore. I was relieved when I came to know virtual meetings were the order of the day—the way forward in the present world order. It didn't take us long to enter our investors' minds.

Our history was new knowledge to them. For the same reason, they were overjoyed. Rather, thrilled. We countered their sense of wonder at a jewellery group coming out with a public issue, after a very long time, with a simple word: 'trust'. Many hands stretched out from all over the world, saying 'We are with you.'

No, the challenges never ended there. Like a bolt from the blue came the news of a second Covid wave. Would the filing of the RHP be hit? The question was uppermost in our minds. It was the moment I realized the answer was not in our hands. It was predestined. What had to happen had to happen. And it happened. In March 2021. On 9 March, amid the Covid scourge, we filed the RHP. The very next day, we got SEBI's final nod. God was leading us to a big victory.

The IPO countdown was for three days, starting 16 March. Much before that, our well-wishers from all over the world began calling and sending us greetings. Those who came to our showrooms congratulated us personally, saying 'Everything will be fine.' Though we were extremely happy, we seemed as tense as Class X students who were waiting to write the board exam. Though we had studied well, a feeling of tension lingered. Our hearts beat fast.

16 March. First day. I felt my heart beat as in a countdown. The results would be known without any delay. For the first two hours, I kept my eyes and ears shut—not wanting to know anything. On the first day itself, the figure we had in our minds came flowing in. What gave us greater joy was the feeling that the people trusted us. Gone was our anxiety for the next two days.

On the second day, we were flooded with calls from all the major stockbrokers. A demat account is essential to buy or sell shares. Lots of people open demat accounts but never use them for various reasons. The brokers called us to say that many demat account holders were frantically trying to renew their accounts! We were speechless when we came to know that people who had not made a single investment in a decade were now making a mad scramble for the share market since Kalyan Jewellers' entry! There were quite a few who made their first foray into the stock market, courtesy of Kalyan.

Shares are listed on the stock exchange a few days after completing their allotment. In India, they are listed on the Bombay Stock Exchange

(BSE) and the National Stock Exchange (NSE). Listing a company's shares on the stock exchange means the shares are ready for trading. A bell is rung symbolically at the exchange building to signal readiness. Our bell ought to have been rung in Mumbai. Unfortunately, the Covid scourge was very high in Mumbai. I was warned against travelling to Mumbai during that period. The bell-ringing ceremony could be held online, said many well-wishers in my team. It was one of the most precious moments in my life and I was not one to give it a miss. There probably may not be another defining moment like this. I decided to go to Mumbai.

26 March 2021. As ever before, this time too, God's will prevailed. Scripting a golden chapter in the annals of Kalyan Jewellers, the bell rang at the National Stock Exchange in Mumbai. Believe me, I did not feel they were my hands that had helped bring us to this moment. I was a mere instrument in the hands of God. When I saw 'Kalyan Jewellers' come bright on the display board, my mind raced back to the time I opened my first shop. It was the same feeling. Of unalloyed joy.

* * *

The IPO period once again proved that God was with us. After we had completed all formalities and the people proudly shared a part of our trust, came the second Covid wave. The lockdown was clamped in several parts of the country. Had we been late by two weeks, all our plans would have gone awry. Our IPO dream would have gathered dust as if caught in some red tape. But that was not to be. I would call it an act of God. His presence made everything possible at the opportune moment, with considerable ease.

Our IPO plan took off in the intervening period of the two Covid waves when the intensity of the first wave was waning and life was returning to normal. Call it a calm before the storm. Or rather, a short break. It was an auspicious moment for us.

We had intended to raise Rs 1100 crore through our public issue. But Kalyan Jewellers raked in Rs 4000 crore. 'Swami, didn't you get three times the amount you had sought for?' Many people asked me that in those days. I knew that the excess amount had to be repaid. Still, that question gave me goosebumps. It meant that the people trusted us three times more than we had expected. Also, it was widely acknowledged. I was in seventh heaven.

With the IPO, our responsibilities increased. Earlier, Kalyan Jewellers belonged to just my children, Warburg and me. Now, it belonged to lakhs of others too. So, we had to be wary at each step. Those who bought our shares hope and pray that Kalyan Jewellers prospers day by day. Only then will they too benefit. The onus is on us to keep that faith. For it is we who are in the driving seat.

The imagery of the car which I talked of in the case of Warburg has changed. It's a train now. We are driving a big train. Lots of people have boarded our train. They have reposed their faith in us, offered us money and undertaken the journey with us. It is our responsibility, ours alone, to see that each one gets to his or her dream destination safely.

The faith that the people have reposed in us is extra sweet. First, they gave us money and bought gold from us. Trusting us to the hilt, they have now invested their hard-earned money in us. The happiness is mutual.

From one person to many people, the journey of trust continues . . .

27

And I Saw Lord Rama

Belief in God is a very personal matter. Some believe, some don't. There may be both believers and non-believers among those who read this book. I respect the beliefs of both.

I am an ardent believer. For the same reason, I'm devoting this entire chapter to my belief in God. For I believe I'd be doing a great dishonour to God if, while writing my autobiography, I didn't pen down God's abundant blessings in my life.

According to Hindu belief, God is worshipped in many forms. I see all forms of God as one. Almost all believers are like this. Yet, many would like to embrace one particular form as their favourite deity.

Ask me who Sri Ramaswamy is, and I won't say that's my favourite deity. My answer would be, more than that, it's the very air that I breathe—the breath of life. Sri Rama, to me, is an unfathomable, unexplainable light source. Not just to me—to my forefathers and now, to my family. All that we have received has come from Sri Ramaswamy—the guardian of the word 'Kalyan'.

I've always felt the presence of Lord Rama from my childhood. It was thus I grew up. I could feel the aura in my home and in the place where Sri Rama stood. I spent my childhood around the Seetha Ramaswamy Temple in the temple village of Pushpagiri in Punkunnam.

My grandfather and father used to go to the Seetha Ramaswamy temple every day. It's a sight I've been seeing ever since I was a kid. I remember being taken to the temple daily before I joined school. Once I joined school, the visits to the temple were only on holidays in the company of my father and grandfather. My friendships and games were all centred around the temple and its precincts.

Chants of 'Rama, Rama . . .' filled my house at all times. In the evenings, my grandfather would make someone read out loud the Ramayana. In his fabulous collection of books, grandfather had different versions of the Ramayana, namely, Valmiki Ramayana, Kamba Ramayanam, Ezhuthachan's Ramayanam . . . Inspired by the great work and drawing its essence, Grandfather wrote his version of the Ramayana. He never published it but treasured it among his collections.

At night, my grandfather would narrate to me stories from the Ramayana. So I grew up seeing Lord Rama right before my eyes and feeling his presence in my heart and soul. Sri Rama Navami, the most important festival of the temple, used to be celebrated with great traditional fervour during our summer vacation. For ten days and nights, a festive yet pious aura would engulf the entire Pushpagiri village. For us children, those were days of great expectation and joy. For we would get new clothes! We used to wear them and go to the temple with great pride.

The deity would be taken out on five elephants and we would stand and watch them. Some elders would take us near the elephants. The mahout's permission was needed to touch the elephant. Our hearts would leap with joy when the mahout gave his nod. With trembling fingers, we would touch the elephant and return home happy and contented.

During festive days, it was the duty of the seniors to draw the chariot bearing the idol of Sri Ramaswamy. It was indeed an ecstatic sight! For ten days, we used to have a sumptuous feast with two payasams (sweet dishes)—a sweet testimony to the grand festival.

Close on the heels of Sri Rama Navami would arrive the festivities of spring in May. The temple precincts would be like a huge, beautiful garden. A huge tank would be filled with water. Ducks would swim about in the water, bringing memories of swans that used to glide elegantly. Beautiful flowers would blend their hues and spread fragrance everywhere. Peacocks, brought from elsewhere, would spread their plumes and dance majestically. The spring festival was a feast for all the five senses.

Prominent personalities from all over India would arrive at the temple to hold programmes at the spring festival. Music maestros Semmangudi and Chembai have graced Pushpagiri with their presence. The people of Thrissur living in faraway places used to throng Pushpagiri to see and hear world-famous musicians and dancers perform at the festival. Many renowned personalities have blessed Pushpagiri with their presence—from yesteryear stalwarts to artistes such as Hariharan, Shankar Mahadevan, Sobhana, Manju Warrier and many more. What brought them all to Pushpagiri was not the remuneration. Rather, it was the blessed opportunity to showcase their talents in this hallowed place. The spring festival at the Seetha Ramaswamy Temple, even to this day, is as colourful as it was in the days of yore. Personalities like Amitabh Bachchan accepted our invitation and graced the festival with their presence.

The forty-five-day 'week' in December is yet another important event at the temple. During these days too, we would be forever in the temple courtyard. Shivaratri too is celebrated here in a big way.

When childhood made way for youth, having a dip in the temple pond and praying at the temple became a habit. As work became hectic at our shop, I failed to find time for this practice. But I made it a point to go to the shop only after circumambulating the temple. It's a habit my father and grandfather taught me, which I continue even to this day. I go to the office only after circumambulating the temple. On

Sundays and public holidays, I enter the temple, have a darshan of the Lord and spend some moments there.

The main deities of the temple are Lord Rama and Sita Devi. As far as I know, I don't think there is any other temple in Kerala having both Lord Rama and Sita Devi together as the main deities. The presence of deities (*upadevatha*) Lakshmana and Hanuman close to Lord Rama and Sita Devi is yet another rarity. Idols of Parvathy and Parameshwaran, Ganapati, Subramanian and Valli Devi, and *navagrahas* and *nagadevatas* lift one's spirits. Inside the temple compound stands another temple with Lord Shiva as the deity. Sandwiched between the main temple and the Shiva temple is a temple dedicated to Lord Ayyappa, whose idol was installed thirty years ago.

Circumambulating the temple is a must before going anywhere. It's a practice that has been going on for several years. The children of Rajesh, Ramesh and Radhika go to school only after circumambulating the temple. In the earlier days, we used to circumambulate the temple in our car before going for official matters. Though the car made way for the chopper, the practice was the same. We undertake each journey in the belief that Sri Ramaswamy will be with us through thick and thin. It's when we have accomplished what we had set out to do that we feel he had been with us throughout our journey.

Our faith in Sri Ramaswamy became firmer with each passing day ever since we began Kalyan Jewellers. He took us to greater heights without a single faltering step. We can stand before him and utter his name only with bowed heads and hands folded in prayer.

As offerings, we have only ourselves to offer before him. Every single second of our life. Yet, we have to make a special offering to the temple. To the faithful, it is of great importance. As jewellers, naturally, it will have a golden touch. We offered a golden flag pole and a golden chariot to the temple.

In 2011, we gave a golden flag pole as an offering to the temple. And in 2013, the golden chariot. It was for the first time in Kerala that a golden chariot was offered to the temple. It took three months for the artisans from Palani to fashion the 15.5-foot-high, 10-foot-wide golden chariot. It was dedicated on 31 March 2013, with great pomp and show. It is in this golden chariot that Sri Ramaswamy circumambulates the village on all the days of the ten-day festival.

We set apart a portion of the returns from our business for Sri Ramaswamy. It has been so since the days of my grandfather. In the second chapter, I mentioned my grandfather offering rice to the temple daily. My grandfather had a textile business. He may have offered rice to the temple as neither clothes nor material could be given as an offering. Today, we deal in gold. Gold can be offered in many forms. We know very well that before Sri Ramaswamy our grandfather's offering of rice has a greater value than our offering of the golden chariot. We hope and pray that the Lord considers our offering too as intense as our grandfather's offering.

Grandfather always considered Lord Rama as the visible god— one we could see and feel at all times. Grandfather had narrated many incidents in his life where he had seen and felt His presence.

My experience proves my grandfather right. Sri Ramaswamy is indeed a very visible god. Only, I haven't said this to anyone except my family members. What if others who heard this disbelieved me? Others don't need to believe in my beliefs. They may consider them outright foolishness.

But now, I feel I should share my experiences with you through this book. These are true incidents. I won't feel offended if they appear unbelievable to you.

It happened before we set out to do business in gold. We approached several banks for a loan when our funds seemed insufficient. No help was forthcoming from anywhere. At night, I couldn't sleep. My thoughts were forever about raising funds. One night, Sri Ramaswamy appeared before me. Was it in my sleep or was I awake? I do not know. One thing was sure. I saw him. 'Fear not,' he said. 'You will get sufficient funds. Your business will be a success.' The words rang in my ears from somewhere. In a split second, all clouds of gloom vanished from my mind.

I had earlier said how GoodKnight Mohan came to my aid when all doors slammed shut before me. I firmly believe it was Sri Ramaswamy who came to me in the guise of Mohan.

My second experience was during the IPO days. It was the time of the Covid scourge. Homes became offices. We had to prepare and send a lot of documents. Discussions were pretty hectic.

D-Day dawned. I'd say it was the IPO Climax Day. It was the last day of the eleven-day struggle. The IPO would be decided according to the investment yardstick of the anchor investors. For this, investments by a lot of anchor investors were necessary. Though we had many credible investors, the deciding factor was a lone investor. Everything depended on his approval. With that, we could confidently announce the IPO. For the past eleven days, we had been toiling hard to get the investments of the anchor investors. If we didn't get the required number, all our efforts would go to waste. The IPO could be a non-starter and would have to be put on the back burner. So, we were all very anxious. Like a Gordian knot, it kept us all on tenterhooks.

We were all at Ramesh's home office. It was dusk. After discussions, Rajesh and I went back to our houses. Ramesh too went inside. A couple of our officials lingered, engaged in discussions.

Finally, everyone dispersed. Ramesh's secretary, Suresh, entered the room to draw the window curtain. What he saw startled him. Sitting on the terrace was a monkey! Suresh never spoke a word of it to anyone. He returned without drawing the curtain.

An hour later, Ramesh came to the room for further discussions after having his bath and prayers. Only a few hours remained for the day to end. Our wait for anchor investors continued. With an anxious mind, Ramesh went to the window and looked out. Sitting on the terrace was a monkey. He showed it to Suresh, who said it had been sitting there for a long time.

The monkey took one look at the faces in the window and disappeared.

Close on the heels of the incident, Rajesh and I entered the room for the next round of meetings. We were blissfully unaware of what had happened. To outsiders, it may be a mere monkey. To us, it was our 'visible god'. What happened at the fifth minute substantiated our belief. Ramesh's phone rang. It was an anchor investor saying he was ready to invest in our company! All our anxieties vanished in a moment. We had the required number of anchor investors. There were no more hurdles. All decks were now clear for the IPO . . .

Ramesh put the phone down and shared with us the good news. It was only then he spoke about seeing the monkey. It was a replica of Lord Hanuman, I felt. It was a messenger sent by none other than Sri Ramaswamy to bless us. My old-fashioned mind believes so even to this day.

'For the past eleven days, I had been offering betel-leaf garlands to Hanuman Swamy,' Ramesh's wife, Deepa, said with folded palms when she heard about the incident.

No one had seen the monkey before. Nor after.

We are confident that Sri Ramaswamy will appear before us whenever we face challenges, whenever we are desperate and whenever we are at a crossroads. Once again, I humbly prostrate before our family's 'visible god'.

'I saw Sita . . .' was what Hanuman told Lord Rama when he returned from Lanka after meeting Sita.

Likewise, I too say I've seen Sri Rama many times in my life.

28

Gratitude Is Not Just a Word

In the past pages, you read about my past and learnt about my present. You may think now I'm going to say something about the future.

I don't think about the future. God decides everything. Nothing can happen beyond that. Man's technical knowledge cannot rewrite what God has written. Man can only wait patiently for God's will to be done.

I do business with gold. What is its future, many have asked me. Gold is mined from ores. What would I do if this supply depletes? Well . . . let such a situation come. God will show the way.

Let me tell you something from my experience. Man's passion for gold will not wane. Rather, it will only increase with each passing day. From the moment I started my first shop, I've been hearing that the demand for gold will decrease in the future. What's interesting is that the demand for gold has only increased year after year.

Earlier, only women wore jewellery. As years passed, men too began wearing jewellery. Today, like women, men too love gold. So, the demand for gold will never diminish.

From time immemorial, gold was a source of attraction and investment. For centuries together, places of worship used to accumulate gold as their asset. A classic example is the Padmanabhaswamy Temple. It is nothing but gold that made it one of the richest temples in the world. The concept of gold in place of money has been in vogue for a very long time.

My sister got married in the 1950s. Gold was a very important factor, even in those days. Land and gold will always appreciate, my grandfather used to say. But there's a difference. It is difficult to sell land when there is an emergency. Gold can easily be sold or exchanged for cash.

In India, a person's association with gold begins when he/she is born. From the first touch of gold on a newborn's tongue to the use of gold to mark each stage of a child's growth and to the day of his/her wedding when they shine as bright as the metal itself.

Gold is part of our culture and is associated with most rituals. It is also one of the most liquid assets.

* * *

The year I was featured on the *Forbes* list for the very first time, I received an invitation for a talk in Mumbai. One question they asked me was, if gold is considered an asset, aren't gold bonds as good as gold? My simple answer was: 'No, because you cannot wear gold bonds on your neck.'

The sentimental value Indians attach to gold is greater than its image as an alternative to currency. Hence, the passion for gold will never wane.

My experience tells me that, after the age of fifty, a lot of philosophical questions and answers will cross your mind. Most often, you will have to explain yourself to others. Especially when you have carved a niche for yourself in this big, wide world. I, too, have had such questions and answers in my mind. And I have had a lot of explaining to do.

As we grow old, our thoughts mature. It's the time when the impulsiveness of youth makes way for consistency. I'm putting aside my pen after writing such thoughts towards the end of my autobiography. Let time fill in the rest of the story.

'Swami, never once have we seen you either upset or angry. How is it possible?' many have asked me. Let me tell you sincerely that neither my business nor the tensions associated with it have affected me. I know it's hard for you to believe. But that's the truth. I never get tense over anything.

The reason? I'm not overambitious. These words come straight from my heart. An industrialist with over a hundred jewellery showrooms all over the world, not ambitious at all! I know you will be surprised. It's a lesson I've learnt. Never be overambitious. That's what my grandfather taught me. Vaulting ambition will lead to your doom. This doesn't mean you shouldn't have desires or be ambitious. Without desires or ambition, life would become meaningless. I have said this in another chapter. It is when you are overambitious that worries crowd your mind. I am satisfied with what I have.

If so, then why do I open more showrooms and seek to expand my business, you may ask. Well . . . I am a jeweller and I do business in gold. With each passing day, I try to perform in a better way than I did the previous day. Don't we all want to succeed in whatever we do? No one wants to be a failure. It's the same way with me too.

Business, to me, is not merely a means to make money. Our forefathers did charity work much before the concept of corporate social responsibility came to be in vogue. They helped the poor and the needy. My family and I, too, follow in their great tradition. Kalyan Jewellers today is not ours alone, it belongs to lakhs of shareholders and their families. Each rupee that Kalyan receives belongs to them too. When we take a step forward, it is not just us who are proud. It makes each of these families proud of our progress too.

* * *

If you ask me whether I have cried in my life, the answer is yes. I cried when my mother passed away. The grief was more than what my heart could bear. My father bid us goodbye after a couple of years. But by then, I had developed a kind of courage to withstand the grief. Time had taught me to hide my tears from the world. So, the tears never came from my eyes. Rather, they welled up in my heart. Never has God brought tears to my eyes. The Merciful God has only filled our family with happiness. Not that we have not known failures. Only, He never made me cry again. This is where the sportsperson in me came to my rescue. My sportsman spirit held me in good stead. Unlike many others, I never used to get angry if I failed in sports and games. Some threw their racket down in despair or hit the ball out of the court. That was not my style. I had conditioned my mind to act level-headedly in the face of failure.

I believe that's the mindset a businessman ought to have. Failures are part of any kind of business. You may lose whatever you have in your hand. But, if you want to find your way back, you must have an unfaltering mind. Venting your ire at objects or people will not help. There is no point in smashing whatever you set your sights on, hurling the phone away or screaming at your co-workers and family members. Such emotional outbursts will not resolve your problems. You must be able to tackle all kinds of situations with a certain level-headedness or maturity. Call it presence of mind. See everything in the spirit of a game. Otherwise, you will die of tension many times over.

By God's grace, I didn't have to face many failures in life. There are a couple of tips on overcoming failures and also not losing one's temper. It is the answer to the oft-asked question: 'Swami, we have not seen you become angry even once.' I call them the five mantras of life.

The foremost is punctuality. Time does not wait for anyone. So, whatever you do, do it within the timeframe. Be punctual. You get angry when you see time running out. Do things systematically in the specified time.

The second most important mantra is making the best use of your money. Use money wisely. I'd call it a fund diversion. If you need Rs 10 for something, you ought to have with you Rs 10. Think twice before borrowing money from someone or availing of a loan from somewhere. The need for Rs 10 may eventually land you in a debt of Rs 10,000! Spend only what you have in your hand.

Be a good listener. Your colleagues may have a lot of news, grievances and complaints to share with you. Most of them may be irrelevant or impossible to be implemented. Give them a patient hearing. They may raise pertinent questions. Lend a ear to them too. The confidence and inspiration that an employee gets from the feeling that his employer is there to listen to his grievances are not insignificant. Rather, it boosts his self-confidence, which becomes beneficial to the company too.

Try not to hurt anyone with your words. It is easy to hurt another but remember, it will take years for the scars to heal. Sometimes, it may remain an open wound. Therefore, old-timers say we cannot take back a released weapon or a spoken word. Also, if you hurt someone with your words, it will do more damage to you than to the other person. For it will keep on worrying you in the recesses of your mind. This will hinder you from taking wise decisions.

Finally, never try to achieve anything by hook or by crook. Do not have the mindset of a conqueror. Remember, you are doing business, not fighting a war with swords and other weapons. Give others the space they deserve. Remember, pride goes before a fall. Do not lose your head in the mad race to succeed. A good businessman should neither be greedy nor be a warrior galloping at breakneck speed to conquer everything he sets sights on. Rather, he should be like the wise and shrewd minister. What about the king, you ask. That's your business, I'd say. It's the responsibility of the minister to lead the king correctly.

It is peace of mind that makes a businessman successful. If the mind is turbulent, like a stormy sea, how can you move forward? The waves will toss and hurl you to the depths of the sea.

Everyone says the world of business is full of tension. I have so far felt no pressure. For I follow the five aforesaid mantras. I live in the present. I am not troubled by the word 'tomorrow'. Be satisfied and happy with the present. You never know about tomorrow, for it is uncertain. Remember, if you brood over what will happen tomorrow, your worries will finally lead to your downfall.

What will you do if one among you goes astray? Will you not lose your control? I can see several people asking me these questions. Let me tell you, all five fingers of the hand are not the same. All the students in a classroom do not have the same calibre. In a game, each of the eleven players has his or her style. So, what does one do? Try to bring the ones who have gone astray or those who don't travel with the flock back to the fold. Never wholly reject the less capable persons. Rather, you must uplift them with the help of capable and efficient ones. Never alienate the ones who have a grouse or pick up a quarrel with you. Rather, win them over to your side. Fight adharma with dharma, not adharma.

Don't dismiss these as the mumblings of an old man. Rather, see them as what life taught a man who does business for a living.

What's your next desire? It's a question anyone who has reached my age may have to encounter. Places one may want to see or the vehicles one may want to acquire—which of these hold a place in your mind?

Well . . . I don't have any such desires. God has given me everything in plenty. He continues to give me everything according to my needs. Let me reiterate: God will take me to the places I want to visit and show me the sights I want to see.

I began as a textile merchant and am now a jewellery retailer. This will be my vocation tomorrow too. I have certain goals to meet. You can consider them to be my expectations from whatever is left of my life.

Kalyan Jewellers has brought several revolutionary changes in the jewellery business scene—everything beneficial to the consumers. I'd consider it like a football tournament. The goal of each team is to win the cup. Opponents will employ all kinds of strategies and skills, some even harsh, at their disposal to win the game. Each player has to survive the odds and win the final. It is for that defining moment that they sweat it out in the field. I am patiently waiting for that day when the business of gold will be as pure as the yellow metal we deal in. What else can a person who lives and swears by the gold that he does business in 24x7 aspire for in the evening of his life?

There is nothing more to be said. Except to express my gratitude for having come thus far. I'm grateful, foremost, to God without whose blessings I wouldn't have been able to write my memories. I feel God's presence at every moment of my life. I prostrate before that heavenly presence—from Sri Ramaswamy to all those forms of God who have appeared before me from time to time.

After God, come my father and mother. I owe it to them for having brought me into this world. Without them, I am no one. My mother's sacrifice began from the day she carried me in her womb for nine months to every stage of my growth into an adult. I was fortunate enough to feel the safety and security of that womb for as long as she was alive. Each day, I lulled myself to sleep in its coolness.

My father was a lighthouse—one who held my hand and showed me the way. My link with my roots begins with a boy named Rama Shastri who came to Kerala from Tamil Nadu. My immediate link was none other than my father. Through him, I saw my great-grandfather and grandfather. I travel back in time as I stand at the end of the family chain that began with Rama Shastri and continued with my father, and realize that I am not alone. I can feel many hands caressing my forehead, blessing me. I feel a sense of inner peace. I pay obeisance to my forefathers.

From the time I began business in the name of Kalyan, my strength has been the people. It is they who held my hand and took me to greater heights. Behind the inception of Kalyan Jewellers is the overwhelming support of the people. From our very first customer at Kalyanram Textiles on Municipal Office Road, Thrissur, to the ones who, till today, go home happily with jewellery from Kalyan Jewellers—I remember everyone with gratitude. I have lost count of the number of people—some I know, many I do not . . . several lakhs.

I hold them all close to me. I hold their hands in mine. I have only this to say: Thanks. Trust me, trust us. It's not just a word. My life and the lives of my family members are your gifts of charity.

I had earlier said Kalyan Jewellers is a huge joint family. There is no need to say thanks to one's family members. Yet, I embrace each one of my colleagues who has helped Kalyan Jewellers grow and take it to greater heights. There are many more miles to go. Let this bonhomie continue.

Let me sign off by thanking the reader for picking up this book to read. I fold my palms before your magnanimous heart. Each word of what I have said is true. Trust me.

Trust. That's all that matters.

Scan QR code to access the
Penguin Random House India website